PURE

Rebecca St. James

with Dale Reeves

PURE

a 90-day devotional for the mind, the body, & the spirit

New York Boston Nashville

All Scripture quotations, unless otherwise indicated, are taken from the HOLY BIBLE, NEW INTERNATIONAL VERSION®. Copyright © 1973, 1978, 1984 by International Bible Society. Used by permission of Zondervan Publishing House. All rights reserved.

Scriptures marked NLT are taken from the *Holy Bible*, New Living Translation, copyright © 1996, 2004. Used by permission of Tyndale House Publishers, Inc., Wheaton, Illinois 60189. All rights reserved.

Scriptures marked THE MESSAGE are taken from *The Message*, copyright © 1993, 1994, 1995, 1996, 2000, 2001, 2002. Used by permission of NavPress Publishing Group.

FaithWords
Hachette Book Group USA
237 Park Avenue
New York, NY 10017

Visit our Web site at www.faithwords.com.

Printed in the United States of America

First Edition: September 2008
10 9 8 7 6 5 4 3 2 1

FaithWords is a division of Hachette Book Group USA, Inc.
The FaithWords name and logo are trademarks of Hachette Book Group USA, Inc.

Library of Congress Cataloging-in-Publication Data
St. James, Rebecca.
  Pure : a 90-day devotional for the mind, the body, and the spirit / Rebecca
  St. James.—1st ed.
    p. cm.
  ISBN 978-0-446-50041-8
  1. Christian women—Religious life. 2. Devotional calendars. I. Title.
  BV4527.S724 2008
  242'.643—dc22   2008012627

I dedicate this book to my mother, Helen, a beautiful example of purity to me. Mum, thank you for modeling what it means to love God with your mind, body, and spirit. You live this book! And thanks for being a wonderful mum. I love you.

Acknowledgments

To Dale Reeves, friend, brother, miracle worker: Thank you is not enough. You bless me and this ministry. I'm grateful.

Thanks to Rolf and Lori and Anne at FaithWords for believing in this message.

Special thanks to Beth and Rick at Alive Communications for your hard work and vision.

Many thanks to Pastor Rick for your faithfulness to Jesus.

And thanks to everyone who has joined arms with us in sharing and living this message of purity in a broken world. Keep shining.

Contents

PURITY OF BODY

PURITY OF SPIRIT

Introduction

It was mid-August and I was performing at Flevo Festival, just outside Amsterdam, Holland. Dutch audiences have been very supportive of my music, singing louder and generally getting involved more than just about anywhere else in the world—so I was expecting a good and encouraging show! To build momentum before I went onstage, a TV crew broadcast a live interview with me from backstage. Then my introduction came and cameras followed me to the stage while the band began to play the first song.

All of a sudden I realized there was a problem. The monitors attached to a pack on my back, which allow me to hear the music, and therefore sing on pitch and in time, were not working properly. A cord had come unplugged somewhere along the way, and with seconds until I needed to go onstage and begin singing, I frantically tried to decide what to do. The old adage "The show must go on" is true, and by the time I went out to the crowd of more than five thousand people, I still hadn't been able to restore my ear monitors. I tried to discreetly fix the problem during the short breaks in the middle of songs, but nothing helped. Finally I got to "Wait for Me," my "purity song" and one I knew I could not professionally pull off without hearing properly. I decided to eat my pride, pull the whole corded mess from the back of my jacket, and explain to the audience what was going on! I laughed it away with a word to them that they were getting to see the behind-the-scenes action . . . onstage!

With the receiver pack hidden in my clothing, the in-ear monitors are practically invisible, but even so, they are the biggest influencers of my actions onstage. In the same way, our internal receivers, the mind and spirit, are what most strongly affect our bodies' actions in life. If they are tuned in to the wrong signal or are not working properly, trouble is on the way. In the area of purity, actions always begin in the hidden places of the heart.

That's why this book exists: to encourage purity from the inside out—to broadcast God's pure way into your mind and heart so you know how to sing His tune, which is far more beautiful than any other! The truths here are designed to help us find and maintain purity of the mind, body, and spirit, for "the pure in heart . . . will see God" (Matt. 5:8).

There are many reasons why I believe purity is so important. I am passionate about purity because it works. I am passionate about purity because it protects me—and my future husband and kids. I am passionate about purity because it is romantic and beautiful. And I am passionate about purity because it makes my Father smile. Many people think of being pure as an action—something they must *do*—rather than approaching it as something they can *be*.

I'm glad you've picked up this book, and that we will take

this journey together. These pages encourage purity as a way of life. Striving to live a pure life physically is itself obviously a huge goal, but in addition, the way you turn over your fears and priorities to God, the way you forgive others, the way you think about every subject in your life—and your life to come—are also part of living a pure life before our Father. That's why in this book you'll find devotions to help you focus on the *total* purity of life. The body, the mind, and the spirit are all designed to be in sync with God's design. When we're living a pure life in every way, it's amazing what happens. How passionate are you about pleasing God and letting nothing cloud your relationship with Him? When living out of love for our Father becomes our biggest passion, our lives are greatly impacted—not only our decisions about how we treat our bodies, but also how we protect and feed our minds and spirits as well.

On each page of this ninety-day journey, you'll read words from God for your daily reflection. Meditating on Scripture helps God's purity become a larger part of our lives. After reading the devotion for the day that's ahead, reflect on the "Looking Further" thoughts. Finally, if you really want God's Word to make a difference in your daily walk, follow through with the "Living It Out" suggestions. This is a great opportunity for God's Word to implant itself in your mind—and purify your life and decisions.

Thanks for joining me on this journey!

Pursuing the PURE life together,

Rebecca St. James

PURITY OF MIND

DAY ONE

In Tune with God's Purpose

God's love is meteoric, his loyalty astronomic, his purpose titanic, his verdicts oceanic. Yet in his largeness nothing gets lost; not a man, not a mouse, slips through the cracks.

—Psalm 36:5–6, THE MESSAGE

Reflection

When I was twelve years old, I attended a program at my school that significantly impacted my life's story. A speaker asked people to come forward if they felt God leading them to give their gifts and talents to Him. I felt led by God to respond and ask for His direction in discovering His will and purpose for my life. It was that same year that God began to lead me into music. At age thirteen, I released my first album in Australia. It was a worship album titled *Refresh My Heart*. I've been asked a number of times, "What do you feel most called to do?" I feel that my God-given purpose is to encourage people to stand for God, to live radically for Him, and to live a life of worship. The roots of this began when I responded to God at age twelve.

This devotional journey is all about seeking purity of mind, body, and spirit. And to seek after purity, we must begin in our minds. One definition for *pure*, when used in the sense of a musical tone, means "free from harshness or roughness and being in tune."[1] God has a purpose for every one of our lives, and He invites us to get in tune with His plan. To be pure is to seek His purpose first and foremost in our lives. If we want our lives to have an impact, that begins and ends with discovering and living out our God-given purpose. Without purpose we have no clear direction, and we may not know which decision to make when we're at a crossroads. Purpose gives us focus to discern what is important. And purpose gives us the strength to do what we need to do. One of this world's greatest tragedies is a life lived without discovering one's God-given purpose. We need to be careful to not just go through the motions without knowing our life purpose. We aren't really living unless we know why we're alive.

Looking Further

Since the beginning of time, God has made everything "on purpose." He created the sky for a reason: to separate the water of the earth from the waters of the heavens (see Gen. 1:6-8). He made the land with a purpose: so there would be dry ground between the seas for us to live on (see Gen. 1:9-12). He designed the sun and the moon with a plan in mind: to mark off seasons, days, and years (see Gen. 1:14-18). And as the crowning glory of creation, He fashioned human beings in His own image (see Gen. 1:26-27). If He thinks highly enough of you and me to put His fingerprint on us, we can be assured that He has a purpose for every one of us. The apostle Paul put it this way:

> Everything, absolutely everything, above and below, visible and invisible . . . everything got started in him and finds its purpose in him. He was there before any of it came into existence and holds it all together right up to this moment. (Col. 1:16-17, THE MESSAGE)

Living It Out

Are you in tune with God's purpose for your life? In order for your dreams and His plan to live in harmony together, you have to cooperate. If you are not on the same page with Him, ask God to show you what He has in mind and to give you the courage to follow His plan. He wants to make the journey with you toward finding the purposeful life for which He destined you.

DAY TWO

Who Determines Your Worth?

What's the price of a pet canary? Some loose change, right? And God cares what happens to it even more than you do. He pays even greater attention to you, down to the last detail—even numbering the hairs on your head! So don't be intimidated by all this bully talk. You're worth more than a million canaries.

—Matthew 10:29-31, THE MESSAGE

Reflection

Several years ago I embarked on a five-week life-changing experience in Switzerland. I needed spiritual, emotional, and physical recuperation, and I found it at L'Abri (which means "shelter"), a community study center where Christians and non-Christians can seek honest answers about God and His purposes for their lives. It was there that the Lord spoke to me of my God-worth to the point that it began replacing my self-worth. Before this experience I don't think I had ever really discovered the sense of wholeness in God that I felt there.

One of the things I had to confront in my life was the issue of perfectionism. When you are a perfectionist, you tend either to push yourself all the time to be better or to go into failure mode and give up, believing that you'll never succeed. My tendency was to live with a sense that God was disappointed in me—that I was not good enough. Through study and prayer and time alone with Him, the Lord assured me that I am loved and secure. I know that I'm His princess, accepted and cherished. *True dat!!*

Yeah I know what you mean.

Because many people spend much of their time trying to please others, they're uncomfortable in their own skin and don't know who they are. Unfortunately, they derive their sense of worth from what they do or don't do for others. It's all based on a false and conditional love. We can get so wrapped up in our selfishness that we can't see beyond ourselves to find our worth in God—who we are in Him.

Looking Further

If you've read *The Lord of the Rings* trilogy by J. R. R. Tolkien, or have seen the movies, you're familiar with the creature Gollum and his obsession with "my precious," the ring. He was willing to do anything to keep it, and went to great lengths in an attempt to reclaim it. Ultimately, his selfish fascination with the treasure cost him his life. Unlike Gollum, God's love for us is purely *selfless* because He was willing to give up what's most important to Him—His only Son—to redeem you. He cherishes you as His precious creation. The apostle Paul put it this way:

> Christ arrives right on time to make this happen. He didn't, and doesn't, wait for us to get ready. He presented himself for this sacrificial death when we were far too weak and rebellious to do anything to get ourselves ready. And even if we hadn't been so weak, we wouldn't have known what to do anyway. We can understand someone dying for a person worth dying for, and we can understand how someone good and noble could inspire us to selfless sacrifice. But God put his love on the line for us by offering his Son in sacrificial death while we were of no use whatever to him. (Rom. 5:6-8, THE MESSAGE)

Living It Out

How much time do you spend in the morning thinking about how others will perceive you based on what you look like each day? How could you spend some of that time contemplating your worth in God's eyes? Look in the mirror and realize how precious you are to Him.

DAY THREE

Faithful Followers

Come, let us worship: bow before him, on your knees before GOD, who made us! Oh yes, he's our God, and we're the people he pastures, the flock he feeds.

—Psalm 95:6-7, THE MESSAGE

Reflection

During our tour of Europe in 2006, we were blessed to be able to visit the Faroe Islands—a windswept archipelago of eighteen islands in the North Atlantic—formerly a possession of Denmark. Many people do not even know this place exists. Halfway between Iceland and Norway, the Faroe Islands are populated by approximately 50,000 people and 70,000 sheep! Several species of whales can be found swimming around the islands.

The people of the Faroe Islands have their own language, the oldest parliament in the world, and unlike most other countries in Europe, the nation is heavily Christian. More than thirty thousand of its inhabitants claim to be born-again believers in a country where abortion is illegal and pornography is prohibited by law. We were blown away to discover these facts about the country. It's almost like God tucked away this people to live a life set apart for Him—and yet, that's what He wants all of us to do, live a life that is radically different from the rest of the world around us.

The root word from which the Faroe Islands derives its name, *Faroese*, literally means "Sheep Islands." How appropriate a name for a people group in which the majority of the population is striving to follow Jesus as Lord. Entire families came to our concert to express their praise to God. It was awesome to see parents and children worshipping together. The night—and these beautiful people—was such a phenomenal blessing to us, etching a special place in our hearts that we will not forget.

Looking Further

Sheep are known to be some of the simplest thinking animals in all of God's creation. They are followers, and they do just fine when they are following the direction of the shepherd who cares for them, feeds them, protects them, and tends to their needs. But they can get themselves into trouble when, out of fear, they react to a startling sound and run away from the safety of the flock, or follow another sheep that has gotten lost.

Developing pure minds begins with making a decision concerning which voice we will follow—the voices we hear all around us telling us to please ourselves first and foremost, to do this and that, not worrying about the consequences; or the voice of our loving Shepherd, telling us to follow only Him, go against the tide of popularity, and make decisions that will impact ourselves and others for eternity. The battle of the mind is fought and won by putting a stake in the ground that says, "I choose to think and act on thoughts that are motivated by my heavenly Father, not the thinking that comes through the negative influences in this world."

The apostle Paul said in Colossians 3:1-2, "If you're serious about living this new resurrection life with Christ, *act* like it. Pursue the things over which Christ presides. Don't shuffle along, eyes to the ground, absorbed with the things right in front of you. Look up, and be alert to what is going on around Christ—that's where the action is. See things from *his* perspective" (THE MESSAGE).

Living It Out

> All of us, like sheep, have strayed away. We have left God's paths to follow our own. Yet the LORD laid on him the sins of us all. (Isa. 53:6, NLT)

Is there a specific area in your life right now in which you have not been faithfully following the Lord's voice? Confess that area to Him, and thank Him that He laid your sins on His Son so that you could be forgiven. Ask for Him to protect and guide you today; then trust Him to do it.

DAY FOUR

What's on Your Mind?

Come close to God, and God will come close to you. Wash your hands, you sinners; purify your hearts, for your loyalty is divided between God and the world.

—James 4:8, NLT

Reflection

There are many things that vie for our attention every day. Working or going to school consumes much of your energy;

Ahh!

you may have others' needs you must tend to, hobbies you'd like to pursue, shopping trips to the mall or outlet stores, conversations on the phone with close friends, e-mail to deal with, and favorite TV shows to watch. How many times have you wished for more than twenty-four hours in a day? It's so easy in the midst of all this busyness to put God on the back burner. *Unfortunate but true*

One of my favorite ways of spending time with God is by just being in His creation and looking around to see how creative, beautiful, and powerful He is in what we see all around us. I have a garden, and I have been indulging my green thumb lately. It's been wonderful to see God's intricate creativity in the uniqueness of the little flowers that grow. I think some of *or runs* my most powerful times with God have been out on walks—in the midst of nature—praising Him for the majesty I see in His creation.

It's impossible for God to purify our minds if we're not hanging out with Him on a regular basis. Our minds dwell on the things that occupy our time. I feel very passionate about the importance of spending daily time with God, seeking Him with all my heart. It's so easy to just go through the motions and become lukewarm, but Revelation 3:16 says if we do that, we're going to be spit out of God's mouth. He'd rather we be hot or cold. A big part of being hot, of being radical for Him, is seeking Him and requesting, "God, speak to my heart." If we humbly come to Him with this heartfelt prayer, He will purify our minds and our hearts. Time with Him every day is essential to His transforming work in our minds.

If we're *not* spending consistent time with Him, we can't expect Him to change us from the inside out. In order to grow, we need to examine all the things that consume our schedules and then be willing to cut something out. We must choose to make time with God a priority. There are always things we can say *no* to. But when we say *yes* to God, powerful things happen!

Looking Further

Just as God was concerned with the purification of the temple in the Old Testament, He desires that we also purify the temple where He dwells today—our hearts and minds. Here are some verses to meditate on as you seek God's purity for your life:

✔ "Because we have these promises, dear friends, let us cleanse ourselves from everything that can defile our body or spirit. And let us work toward complete holiness because we fear God" (2 Cor. 7:1, NLT).

✔ "He offered himself as a sacrifice to free us from a dark, rebellious life into this good, pure life, making us a people he can be proud of, energetic in goodness" (Titus 2:14, THE MESSAGE).

✔ "If that animal blood and the other rituals of purification were effective in cleaning up certain matters of our religion and behavior, think how much more the blood of Christ cleans up our whole lives, inside and out. Through the Spirit, Christ offered himself as an unblemished sacrifice, freeing us from all those dead-end efforts to make ourselves respectable, so that we can live all out for God" (Heb. 9:13-15, THE MESSAGE).

Living It Out

In a notebook, record how you spend your hours in a typical day. What things are essential? What things are nonessential?

Are you happy with the amount of time you spend with God on a daily basis? If not, what can you cut out of your routine in order to spend more time with Him? Now it's just a matter of following through with your plan. Do it, and watch God transform your mind.

DAY FIVE

A New Season

Forget about what's happened; don't keep going over old history. Be alert, be present. I'm about to do something brand-new. It's bursting out! Don't you see it? There it is! I'm making a road through the desert, rivers in the badlands.
—Isaiah 43:18-19, THE MESSAGE

Reflection

A few years ago, I learned the hard way that it's very important for people in ministry to take time out and be still. I recently took an extended sabbatical and truly focused on praying and seeking God concerning what this time should look like. My life is pretty much mapped out with touring, book writing, songwriting, and time spent in the studio. A sabbatical is a time of open space to approach God with open hands and heart and say, "God, renew me; speak to me; prepare my heart for new things You want to do in my heart and in my ministry." I really have a sense of anticipation that God is moving me into a new "room" of my life—that I have actually been in one room for some time and He is moving me into another space in the house of my life.

I'm very excited about this coming season. God is already opening new doors of ministry! I'm even exploring film and acting opportunities, something I have been wanting to do for some time. It feels to me like a season of newness, and I think this sabbatical is a key to that. Ultimately, I always want to be in the center of God's will and involved in the adventure He has for me.

Feels like that all the time of late

What about you? Do you feel that you are in the center of God's will? Or are you at a place in your life in which your walk with God seems stagnant? Do you long for Him to do something brand-new? The first step is to express that desire to Him. Then sit and be still and listen to God. If you are sensitive to His will and want to find His best for you, you can be assured that He will respond.

Looking Further

Often we think of new beginnings on January 1, but God is about the business of newness far more frequently than that. God is a God of new things. Multiple times in the Psalms, David urges us to "sing to the LORD a new song":

- In Psalm 40:3, David proclaimed, "He has given me a new song to sing, a hymn of praise to our God. Many will see what he has done and be astounded. They will put their trust in the LORD" (NLT).
- Psalm 98:1 says, "Sing a new song to the LORD, for he has done wonderful deeds. His right hand has won a mighty victory; his holy arm has shown his saving power!" (NLT).

✓ And the Bible tells us heaven will be a place filled with new songs (see Rev. 5:9; 14:3).

There are many good songs already in existence. Why is God so concerned with new ones? Because they arise out of new experiences, new ways in which God has recently revealed Himself in our lives. If you've made mistakes that have written a song of failure in your heart, you can find hope in these verses of Scripture. He's not just the God who did some amazing things in our past—He's the God who is doing some amazing things now! And because He is the Creator, He knows how to invent newness in the lives of His children. He simply wants us to come to Him and ask for new times of refreshing.

Living It Out

Do you feel as if you're in a spiritual rut? Have you allowed yourself to settle into a state of apathy or mediocrity, because the same old songs drone on in your life? All you have to do is ask, "God, what new thing do You want to do in my life this season?" If you are willing to ask, He is willing to answer. What are you waiting for? Do it today.

DAY SIX

Praying Through the Pain

Seventy years are given to us! Some even live to eighty. But even the best years are filled with pain and trouble; soon they disappear, and we fly away.

—Psalm 90:10, NLT

Reflection

I have five brothers, and through the years we've watched and played a lot of sports—from swimming to baseball to football. There's a saying in sports when it gets tough for an athlete to compete due to an injury of some sort. The athlete must learn to "play through the pain." I think when it comes to some of the inner pain we all deal with, a good solution is to "*pray* through the pain." God already knows everything about us, and He knows what we're going through at a given moment. He wants us to come to Him recognizing that we need Him in order to persevere through the pain.

If I'm on tour and struggling with something, and am feeling weak—even if I am upset, I have to go onstage with a smile on my face. No one can really take my place in that moment. Every woman feels that at times, whether it's a mom trying to get her rowdy kids into church or a wife who just got into a fight with her husband and now has to walk into the church service or a professional who just got terrible news and has to walk into a meeting or a student who has to give a presentation when her mind is consumed with something else. . . . We put pressure on ourselves to not show on the outside what's happening on the inside.

That's why it is so important to have people in our lives who can really be trusted, and a God who redeems every part of our lives—the mountains as well as the valleys. I need to be able to cry and vent and share the ugly-but-honest truths about myself with my inner circle, and I am doing that more than ever before. It's difficult sharing the hard stuff with God or with other people, letting them see the part of you that you're not proud of. But you've got to.

Jesus understands our pain because He's been there. He became flesh and blood by being born in human form. Hebrews 2:16-18 tells us, "It's obvious, of course, that he didn't go to all this trouble for angels. It was for people like us, children of Abraham. That's why he had to enter into every detail of human life. Then, when he came before God as high priest to get rid of the people's sins, he would have already experienced it all himself—all the pain, all the testing—and would be able to help where help was needed" (THE MESSAGE).

What an awesome thought. He entered into "every detail" of life. And He knows how to pray through pain.

Looking Further

When the Israelites were in bondage in Egypt, they cried out to the Lord in pain. They persistently asked for deliverance from their harsh slave masters. God rescued them. But then they grumbled about many things in the wilderness, such as food, water, and why they had been led there to die. God listened to their complaints and continued to deliver them. His Word says:

I know all about their pain. And now I have come down to help them, pry them loose from the grip of Egypt, get them out of that country and bring them to a good land with wide-open spaces, a land lush with milk and honey. (Exod. 3:7-8, THE MESSAGE)

I took the world off your shoulders, freed you from a life of hard labor. You called to me in your pain; I got you out of a bad place. I answered you from where the thunder hides, I proved you at Meribah Fountain. (Ps. 81:6-7, THE MESSAGE)

Living It Out

I am suffering and in pain. Rescue me, O God, by your saving power. (Ps. 69:29, NLT)

When you're dealing with some kind of private pain, to whom do you go for comfort? Air it out in prayer. God stands ready to hear and to rescue.

DAY SEVEN

Removing the Mask

Watch yourselves carefully so you don't get contaminated with Pharisee yeast, Pharisee phoniness. You can't keep your true self hidden forever; before long you'll be exposed. You can't hide behind a religious mask forever; sooner or later the mask will slip and your true face will be known. You can't whisper one thing in private and preach the opposite in public.

—Luke 12:1-3, THE MESSAGE

Reflection

When I was a little girl growing up in Australia, my brothers and I put on performances for our parents. We'd often pretend to be a rock band. I'd get my hairbrush out and be the lead singer, and they'd bang on the pots and pans. I think we even sold merchandise to our parents during those rock concerts! I also loved to dance to different Christian songs, so I suppose I've always been a bit of a performer.

I remember signing my recording contract at the age of fifteen in the living room of my house in Brentwood, Tennessee. I knew it was a significant moment. I don't think I had any idea just how significant it would really be! I could never have imagined all the aspects of the journey God was about to take me on. It's definitely been an incredible adventure.

One of the things I'm most uncomfortable with in this career is the tendency for people to put Christian performers on a pedestal. It's something my mum calls "the power of the stage."

There are no stars but Jesus—the rest of us are all human. I've always tried to break down the walls and be very real with the people who come to my concerts. So I'm still surprised every now and then when girls come up to me and are really emotional about meeting me. I try to reassure them that I'm just like them—that "we all put our pants on the same way," as the saying goes!

For a long time I thought people shouldn't see my flaws. I thought that when I was going through a tough time I just needed to buck up and be strong; I needed to put on a brave face and just get through it alone. But I've found out otherwise. When you take off the mask (the brave face), you relate at a base level to everyone else who has been through pain—and everyone has. Honesty promotes intimacy, and intimacy encourages our mutual reliance on God. True honesty is beautiful.

Looking Further

The origin of the word *hypocrite* comes from the Greek word that literally means "a stage actor . . . one who pretends to be what he is not."[2] The two masks that still represent theater today, the comedy and tragedy masks, originally had a purpose. Because all actors during the golden age of Greece (500–300 BC) were male, they had to play multiple roles. The masks gave them the ability to change character and mood.

Jesus had some pretty strong words for the play actors, the hypocrites, of His day. They were more concerned with the way they appeared on the outside—how they looked in their giving to the needy, praying in the synagogues, and in denying themselves through fasting—than in what should have been happening in their hearts (see Matt. 6:1-18). About them Jesus said:

"Isaiah was right when he prophesied about you hypocrites; as it is written: 'These people honor me with their lips, but their hearts are far from me. They worship me in vain; their teachings are but rules taught by men'" (Mark 7:6-7).

"What sorrow awaits you teachers of religious law and you Pharisees. Hypocrites! For you are so careful to clean the outside of the cup and the dish, but inside you are filthy—full of greed and self-indulgence! You blind Pharisee! First wash the inside of the cup and the dish, and then the outside will become clean, too. What sorrow awaits you teachers of religious law and you Pharisees. Hypocrites! For you are like whitewashed tombs—beautiful on the outside but filled on the inside with dead people's bones and all sorts of impurity" (Matt. 23:25-27, NLT).

Living It Out

What masks do you have a tendency to wear? Do you ever find yourself acting one way with certain people and a completely different way around others? God calls you to walk consistently, allowing your actions to mirror what's going on in your heart. Get rid of the mask and be real with God, yourself, and others.

DAY EIGHT

In Awe

Since we are receiving a Kingdom that is unshakable, let us be thankful and please God by worshiping him with holy fear and awe. For our God is a devouring fire.

—Hebrews 12:28-29, NLT

Reflection

When I was five or six years old, my family and I attended Thornleigh Baptist Church in Sydney, Australia. That particular church holds special memories for me because it is where I gave my life to Jesus. I remember one Sunday we were singing worship songs in church and I looked up at my mum, who was standing beside me. I saw tears streaming down her cheeks. I asked her why she was crying, and she said there was nothing wrong—she was just worshipping Jesus. In that moment, she taught me a huge lesson about the power of worship, one I don't believe I will ever forget.

Although I didn't really understand it then, I now see why she was crying those tears of joy. I've since experienced worship like that and have responded in the same way. I might be worshipping God in my church or in the middle of a concert when tears fill my eyes or start rolling down my cheeks. There's something very extraordinary that happens when the body of Christ comes together corporately to give honor to God. We stand in awe of His character, His wonders, and His blessings in our lives. Sometimes the sheer power of that moves me to tears. My mum taught me to love Jesus, to stand in awe of Him, and to express my praise. Worship is delighting in God, whether through music, words, or even tears.

Looking Further

To be in awe is to be overwhelmed by God's majesty. David proclaimed, "Because of your unfailing love, I can enter your house; I will worship at your Temple with deepest awe" (Ps. 5:7, NLT). The concept of being in awe seems to be lost today. We are in awe of practically nothing. In our culture we've overused the word *awesome.* In the Old Testament it originally referred to something that was "terrible" or "dreadful," something to be feared. It signified a holy reverence before God, because He is a devouring fire.

The patriarch Jacob dreamed of a stairway that reached from earth to heaven, with angels going up and down on it. At the top of the stairway God appeared and spoke to Jacob about his inheritance and his future descendants. When Jacob arose from his sleep, he declared, "'GOD is in this place—truly. And I didn't even know it!' He was terrified. He whispered in awe, 'Incredible. Wonderful. Holy. This is God's House. This is the Gate of Heaven'" (Gen. 28:16-17, THE MESSAGE). Jacob named the site Bethel, which means "house of God," for it was a holy place of awe-inspired worship.

Exodus 14:30-31 records that after God delivered the Israelites out of bondage, led them safely through the Red Sea, and drowned the Egyptian pursuers, "Israel looked at the Egyptian dead, washed up on the shore of sea, and realized the tremendous power that GOD brought against the Egyptians. The people were in reverent awe before GOD and trusted in GOD and his servant Moses" (THE MESSAGE). On a day when the prophet Samuel called on the Lord, and He responded with thunder and rain, the people were greatly afraid and stood in awe of the Lord (see I Sam. 12:18). There were numerous times in the New Testament after Jesus performed miracles that the crowds were "filled with awe" and expressed their praise to God (see Matt. 9:8; Luke 1:65; 5:26; 7:16).

Living It Out

When was the last time God did something really *awesome* in your life? What can you do to stand in awe of God, in the truly biblical sense of the word? He is worthy of your awe-inspired praise today.

DAY NINE

Bargaining with God

Don't bargain with God. Be direct. Ask for what you need. This isn't a cat-and-mouse, hide-and-seek game we're in. If your child asks for bread, do you trick him with sawdust? If he asks for fish, do you scare him with a live snake on his plate? As bad as you are, you wouldn't think of such a thing. You're at least decent to your own children. So don't you think the God who conceived you in love will be even better?

—Matthew 7:7-11, THE MESSAGE

Reflection

When I go on a shopping excursion, I love hunting for great deals. What girl doesn't love the adventure of finding the best clothing or the coolest decorations for the best price? I think it's part of our DNA as females. A few years ago I bought a house and named it "Avonlea," after a town in one of my favorite books, *Anne of Green Gables*. I want my home to be an eclectic, comfortable, and welcoming space in which to relax. When shopping for furniture, I bought most of the pieces second-hand. I love finding just the right accessory when I'm on the search for something to add to my home decor. And if it's a bargain, I get all the more excited!

No wonder it's easy at times for us females to approach God and try to bargain with Him. In our hearts, we know that He knows what's best for us, yet we tend to be concerned with what the whole "deal" looks like. Sometimes the fear of not knowing everything He has planned keeps us from giving our dreams to Him. We may not say these words, but we may be thinking them: *God, I'll do this if You'll do this. I'll give You this if You'll give it back to me the way I want it.* He's the Lord of the universe, yet sometimes we act as if we can manipulate Him! But God already knows our human ways. And He wants more than that when we approach Him in prayer.

It really all comes down to a matter of trust. God wants us to live fulfilled lives. He wants to shower us daily with His extravagant love. He is *not* withholding good things from us. He desires that we come to Him in obedience—pure and simple. And if we do that, we will be free, and that's what He most wants us to be. I can't think of a better deal anywhere.

Looking Further

The Old Testament wisdom books offer some great insight into this theme of accepting from God what He wants to give us rather than bargaining with Him. We may not always understand what God is up to in our lives, but we can be assured that He's all about what's good for us.

"After looking at the way things are on this earth, here's what I've decided is the best way to live: Take care of yourself, have a good time, and make the most of whatever job you have for as long as God gives you life. And that's about it. That's the human lot. Yes, we should make the most of what God gives, both the bounty and the capacity to enjoy it, accepting what's given and delighting in the work. It's God's gift! God deals out joy in the present, the *now*" (Eccl. 5:18-20, THE MESSAGE).

🦋 "Let your love dictate how you deal with me; teach me from your textbook on life. I'm your servant—help me understand what that means, the inner meaning of your instructions" (Ps. 119:124-125, The Message).

Living It Out

Do you spend more time in prayer asking God for His guidance, attempting to bargain with Him, or simply coming to Him in obedience? Make a concerted effort in your prayer time today to leave the bargaining out, and willful obedience in.

Day Ten

🦋

Called to Worship

Shout joyful praises to God, all the earth! Sing about the glory of his name! Tell the world how glorious he is. Say to God, "How awesome are your deeds! Your enemies cringe before your mighty power. Everything on earth will worship you; they will sing your praises, shouting your name in glorious songs."

—Psalm 66:1-4, NLT

Reflection

There is a worship revolution happening around the world right now. People's hunger for worship is obvious almost everywhere I go. I am extremely fortunate that I get to enjoy some pretty profound worship experiences . . . like the time a few years ago I was in front of sixty thousand people at a large music festival. I was singing an a cappella worship song with the crowd, and as I looked out from the stage onto this vast sea of faces, I was suddenly struck by the effect. I was quite overwhelmed by the moment, just in awe of God and how we could worship Him together like that. It was like a momentary preview of heaven to me. That was awesome.

I believe worship is the greatest thing we can do here on earth . . . and it's one of the things that will continue in heaven! Worship is our calling; it's what we're created to do. I love worshipping God. There is such a need for it today. I define worship simply as our love response to God's love for us. When we express our love to God, when we open ourselves up to the reality of how much He truly loves us, living radically for Him simply becomes a natural lifestyle. It's so much more than going through the motions and just going to church on Sunday and Wednesday and saying, "I'm a Christian." It's living for God 24-7.

God didn't make us robots. He gave us a choice. Every time we choose to worship Him it delights Him, but it's an enjoyable experience for us too. It's an amazing thing to be able to worship the Creator of the universe and feel His pleasure when we do. One of the things that is so excellent about worship is that it really gets our eyes off ourselves and focused on God. When we lead or participate in worship, none of us are called to be a star—God has called us to be servants.

Looking Further

To worship God is to be overwhelmed by His greatness and glory. The concept is so huge that God used several different words in the Bible to express all the manifestations of worshipping Him. In the Old Testament, the Hebrew word *halal* refers to a loud and demonstrative celebration of praise, a joyful shouting. Another word for praise, *yadah*, literally means "to stretch out the hands." Rather than sitting on your hands, or complaining about all that is bad in life, God calls you to release all your burdens to Him with open and outstretched hands, losing yourself in the experience of worshipping only Him. The word *shachah* expresses reverence toward God as we physically bow down before Him. The word *barak* means, "to bless, kneel, salute." It is an act of adoration. The most frequent word for worship in the New Testament is *proskuneo*, which means "to kiss toward." It signifies leaning toward God in an intimate way.[3] This is by no means an exhaustive list of all the words used for worship in God's Word, but it provides a glimpse of the magnitude of the worship we can bring to Him.

Living It Out

What kind of worship is appropriate for you to bring to God today? Joyful exuberance, thankful devotion, humble adoration, or reverent silence? God will delight in any of these offerings from your lips and from your heart. Think about who He is. Praise Him for His faithfulness and constancy. Praise Him for His creation and for His blessings in your life. Then sing a worship song to Him.

Write

DAY ELEVEN

Free Thinking

When God is personally present, a living Spirit, that old, constricting legislation is recognized as obsolete. We're free of it! All of us! Nothing between us and God, our faces shining with the brightness of his face. And so we are transfigured much like the Messiah, our lives gradually becoming brighter and more beautiful as God enters our lives and we become like him.

—2 Corinthians 3:17-18, THE MESSAGE

Reflection

If you look up the word *pure* in Webster's dictionary, you'll find several definitions. Most often we think of purity as describing someone whose life is marked by chastity, someone who is morally pure. But the word means so much more. One of the first definitions is this: "unmixed with any other matter" (as in *pure* gold). Another definition that I really like contains this thought: "*free* from what weakens or pollutes; containing nothing that does not properly belong."[4]

To be pure in your thoughts means that you are striving to stay singularly focused on pleasing God and walking in His ways, thinking only thoughts that *belong* in the mind of a follower of Christ. It's a tall order, no doubt. But it's not about being rigidly tied to God's rules. It's about being free to have an intimate relationship with Him because of His extravagant love for us. Lately I've been learning about the freedom I have in Him—freedom to embrace life because He has set me free.

At times I have been weighed down by expectations of myself that have gone beyond God's requirements of me. Jesus spoke about the Pharisees who burdened themselves and others with rules that were way too strict. I have been guilty of placing these heavy mantles of burden upon myself. All the while, God wanted to free me from the weight of my own expectations and let me know that as long as I submit everything to Him, that's all that matters. I'm learning I can just revel in the freedom He's given me. What a relief! AMEN.

Looking Further

God's guidelines for our lives come from a loving Father who knows us best and wants to protect us from ourselves. The guilt we feel when we disobey God's directives impacts our relationship with Him. That's what grieves God the most—not that we have fallen short of His will for our lives, but that we've pulled away from intimacy with Him! When Adam and Eve initially sinned in the Garden of Eden, they ran and hid from Him. How easy it is for us to do the same. But God has freed us from having to feel that kind of shame by taking all our guilt and placing it on Jesus on the cross for us. Now we obey Him not because of fear, but out of love and gratitude.

Jesus said, "You will know the truth, and the truth will set you free." The Jews answered Him, "We are Abraham's descendants and have never been slaves of anyone. How can you say that we shall be set free?" Jesus replied, "I tell you the truth, everyone who sins is a slave to sin. Now a slave has no permanent place in the family, but a son belongs to it forever. So if the Son sets you free, you will be free indeed" (John 8:32-36).

Living It Out

Are there any areas in your life in which you've been living in bondage instead of in freedom? Our Lord promises to bring healing and grace if we will sincerely cry out to Him. Psalm 118:5-6 states, "In my anguish I cried to the LORD, and he answered by setting me free. The LORD is with me; I will not be afraid. What can man do to me?" When you come to realize what Jesus has released you from, when you no longer view following Him as simply obeying a set of rules, you can "go for it" in life with reckless abandon for God. What expectations of yourself do you need to let go of today so that you can think and live freely?

DAY TWELVE

What Do You Crave?

My soul is starved and hungry, ravenous!—insatiable for your nourishing commands.

—Psalm 119:20, THE MESSAGE

Reflection

One of the greatest blessings God has given His children to enjoy is the wide variety of foods that exist on the earth. When I travel internationally, I sample many different foods from various countries. I also enjoy cooking at home and have lately had a lot of fun making paninis, crepes, scones, and crumpets for friends and family. I even enjoyed an English high tea recently, complete with cucumber sandwiches! Some of my favorite foods are Thai curry, garden omelets, and yogurt. I eat pretty healthy because I've learned that if I eat whatever I want, I'll pay the consequences for it. I try to be wise about my food choices, although I'm not as disciplined as I would like to be. Every now and then I get kind of a sweet tooth that I try to hold back. Like most women, I tend to eat more—and eat things that aren't necessarily good for me—when I'm stressed or feeling a bit off balance.

Spiritually speaking, we are what we eat. We are what we feed on, what we fill our minds with. Sometimes we mentally survive on "junk food" and then wonder why we're not growing in Christ, why we're not maturing beyond some of our same old struggles. Meditate on the sustenance found in God's Word; then pray, "Help me resist the temptation to fill my mind with things that are not healthy to my spiritual nourishment. Give me a distaste for evil and a desire for more of You." *Me too.*

I love to journal as a way of savoring what God is teaching me. There's something very clarifying about putting my thoughts on paper or on the computer. It helps to be able to look back from time to time and see the things I've learned and the progress I've made. When God teaches me something profound, I try to journal so I will remember it. That's a great way to feed the mind things that are good.

Looking Further

After God delivered the Israelites from Egypt and they had wandered in the wilderness for a while, they complained to Moses and craved the foods they had once eaten in Egypt. God had supplied manna (His wonder bread) for them every morning, but in their minds it wasn't enough. They got tired of it and craved meat (see Num. 11). God was displeased with their attitude of ungratefulness. They were busy worrying about what they were going to eat rather than craving God and realizing that He would take care of all their needs. Psalm 78 reveals God's reaction to their thanklessness:

> They ate till they had more than enough, for he had given them what they craved. But before they turned from the food they craved, even while it was still in their mouths, God's anger rose against them; he put to death the sturdiest among them, cutting down the young men of Israel. (Ps. 78:29-31)

God wants us to be grateful and to hunger for Him and His Word more than anything else we could desire physically or spiritually. First Peter 2:2-3 instructs us: "Like newborn babies, you must crave pure spiritual milk so that you will grow into a full experience of salvation. Cry out for this nourishment, now that you have had a taste of the Lord's kindness" (NLT).

If we come to God with a soul craving, He will satisfy all our needs. He promises:

> Open your mouth and taste, open your eyes and see—how good GOD is. Blessed are you who run to him. Worship GOD if you want the best; worship opens doors to all his goodness. Young lions on the prowl get hungry, but GOD-seekers are full of God. (Ps. 34:8-10, THE MESSAGE)

Living It Out

What do you spend more time thinking and chewing on than anything else? To feed your mind things that honor God, what do you need to do less of? Tell God today that you want to hunger for Him more than anything else. Ask Him to satisfy your spiritual needs, and then believe that He will.

DAY THIRTEEN

No Fear

God is love. When we take up permanent residence in a life of love, we live in God and God lives in us. This way, love has the run of the house, becomes at home and mature in us, so that we're free of worry on Judgment Day—our standing in the world is identical with Christ's. There is no room in love for fear. Well-formed love banishes fear. Since fear is crippling, a fearful life—fear of death, fear of judgment—is one not yet fully formed in love.

—1 John 4:16-18, THE MESSAGE

Reflection

I know God does not want me to worry and live in fear, yet there have been seasons in my life in which I felt I was giving in to fear way too much. As a result, I wasn't thriving, I was simply *surviving*. Survival mode for me could be defined as simply getting through and not failing. The majority of my energies were focused on surviving one challenge to get to the next one, simply accomplishing what was before me. It has taken quite some time for me to wake up to the reality that this is not the mind-set God intends for me. He doesn't want me to just survive. He wants me to live with a passion for Him and for others.

At times I have been apprehensive about getting close to guys, largely because doing so involves the potential of hurting someone and being hurt myself. I have been very thankful for my calling and ministry, but it's also made a "normal" romantic life nearly impossible, which kept me from confronting my fear for quite a few years. Over time, though, I've come to grips with the fear of being vulnerable with someone, and along with that the possibility of being hurt. I've had a pretty wonderful life in which there hasn't been much rejection. The possibility of rejection is something that all of us struggle with at some stage, and I have felt the grip of insecurity tighten around me many times. But then I'm reminded that perfect love casts out fear. God is in control, and there's no reason to fear failing in this area of life.

Yes. You understand. This is me too.

I also feel apprehensive almost every time I'm writing songs for a new album. I want them to be just right, so if I'm not careful I can spend way too much time agonizing over the process. When we get into the studio, I have to trust that God has been in it all along and has assembled the right members of the creative team to do what He wants to accomplish. Often while recording, I have been pushed by a producer in a creative direction, and the result has been that some things were pulled out of me that I didn't know were there. I've had to step out of my comfort zone to continue to push the envelope, seeking to do things differently.

Whether in our profession or our relationships, we need to abandon our own self-absorbed thoughts and trust the ultimate *producer*—God. He is for us, and He wants us to thrive!

Looking Further

If fear is not of God, then its source must come from the enemy. It is one of the greatest weapons that he uses to discourage the people of God. He desires that we spend time focusing on our fears and anxieties, rather than trusting the God who loves us and then giving our fears over to Him. God has promised us through the prophet Isaiah, "Don't be afraid, for I am with you. Don't be discouraged, for I am your God. I will strengthen you and help you. I will hold you up with my victorious right hand" (Isa. 41:10, NLT).

Living It Out

Before He left them and returned to His Father in heaven, Jesus promised His disciples, "I am leaving you with a gift—peace of mind and heart. And the peace I give is a gift the world cannot give. So don't be troubled or afraid" (John 14:27, NLT). What fears and apprehensions do you need to lay at the feet of Jesus today? God's perfect love can help banish those fears. Ask Him to help you overcome the negative thoughts that the enemy hurls into your mind. Then express your trust in God's care by letting go of your fears and worries.

DAY FOURTEEN

Questioning God

As the heavens are higher than the earth, so are my ways higher than your ways and my thoughts than your thoughts. As the rain and the snow come down from heaven, and do not return to it without watering the earth and making it bud and flourish, so that it yields seed for the sower and bread for the eater, so is my word that goes out from my mouth: It will not return to me empty, but will accomplish what I desire and achieve the purpose for which I sent it.

—Isaiah 55:9-11

Reflection

I don't think I've ever doubted that Christianity fit me or necessarily wanted to cast it off. But I have questioned God a lot, asking, "Why did You choose to allow this?" and "What are You doing right now?" and "Why do You seem so far away?" The longer I am a Christian, the more I realize God can handle my questions. He can handle my anger; He can handle my hurt.

As Christians, I believe God is always retooling the way we think. God wants us to share our whole hearts with Him—not to share just the parts we think He wants to hear. Sometimes, like David in the Psalms, we share the anxious, hurting thoughts and then resolve them with praise. We often feel like we need to be positive all the time and say that life is great when really it isn't—it's challenging. I think of David being "a man after God's own heart," and David was one who asked God the hard stuff. The Psalms are filled with his questions.

The book of Job is full of questions too. Job was a righteous, God-fearing man of integrity. Yet God gave Satan permission to test Job to see if he would be faithful to his God. Job had seven sons and three daughters, and in one day, all of them were killed. It's impossible for us to imagine that, and perhaps even more impossible to comprehend Job's response to the calamity. In an act of intense grief, Job tore his robe, shaved his head, fell to the ground in worship, and said, "Naked I came from my mother's womb, and naked I will depart. The LORD gave and the LORD has taken away; may the name of the LORD be praised" (Job 1:20-21). I love worshipping God with the song "Blessed Be Your Name," written by Matt and Beth Redman, which is based on this verse.

Even though we don't understand why God allows certain things to occur, as Job found out in a dramatic way, God is still God. He can handle our praise as well as our hurts. He can handle our needs as well as our thanksgiving. Part of being worshipful is being very real about what's going on in our hearts. We can share our angst as well as our adoration and know that God is capable of receiving us before Him in total honesty.

Looking Further

For Job, it got much worse before it got better. He suffered with painful sores from the soles of his feet to the top of his head, and his wife urged him to just curse God and die. He had three friends who came to try to figure out why he was suffering so greatly. They attempted to explain Job's misfortune and offer their comfort, but their counsel was not really of much use to Job. Then, after thirty-five chapters of dialogue between Job and his friends, the Lord spoke. He asked, "Who is this that darkens my counsel with words without knowledge? Brace yourself like a man; I will question you, and you shall answer me" (38:2-3). Then for the next three chapters God asked some powerful questions like these:

- "Where were you when I laid the earth's foundation?" (38:4).
- "Have you ever given orders to the morning, or shown the dawn its place?" (38:12).
- "Can you bring forth the constellations in their seasons or lead out the Bear with its cubs?" (38:32).
- "Does the eagle soar at your command and build his nest on high?" (39:27).

As you question God, do so with a view toward knowing that even though you don't understand the complexities of life, you can know that the One who created everything you see has not abandoned you. He is still in control. Blessed be His name.

Living It Out

What questions do you have for God today? Take a few minutes to read Job 38–41. Your questions may not seem quite as important after that. Even so, be honest with God. He can handle it.

DAY FIFTEEN

Mind Protection

Get rid of all the filth and evil in your lives, and humbly accept the word God has planted in your hearts, for it has the power to save your souls.

—James 1:21, NLT

Reflection

While my six siblings and I were growing up, my parents placed a sign on top of our television that served as a great reminder to watch what we put into our minds. It said, "I will live with a pure heart in my own home. I will not put anything wicked before my eyes" (see Ps. 101:2–3).

What do you spend the majority of your leisure time thinking about? We can prevent a great deal of trouble in our lives by guarding what we put in our minds. In this culture we live in, that can be a daily challenge. We need to be really wise about the magazines we read, what we look at on the Internet, see on TV and in movies, and the music we allow to invade our minds. What goes into our hearts and our minds is going to come out in our lives. We need to ask for God's strength to say *no* to the harmful things that are readily available to us. In order to go against the grain of what is so prevalent, we must spend time in God's Word and ask Him to purify and renew our minds.

If there are images in your mind that you wish weren't there, how can you clean the cobwebs out and get rid of those bad memories? Sincerely ask God to do a thorough house-cleaning in your life. Even though you may remember things you shouldn't have seen or done, in God's mind He has forgotten them. The Bible says in Psalm 103:11–12, "As high as the heavens are above the earth, so great is his love for those who fear him; as far as the east is from the west, so far has he removed our transgressions from us." He has erased our past sins from His memory. Now it's time to move on. We can't change the past, but we *can* control the future—and we know who holds it!

Looking Further

Another way to look at the battle for controlling the mind is by imagining that you have two dogs in your house that you can feed every day. You get to choose which dog you feed more on a daily basis. The apostle Paul spoke about the struggle between the sinful nature and the Spirit in Romans 6–8. He said in Romans 8:5–9:

> Those who live according to the sinful nature have their minds set on what that nature desires; but those who live in accordance with the Spirit have their minds set on what the Spirit desires. The mind of sinful man is death, but the mind controlled by the Spirit is life and peace; the sinful mind is hostile to God. It does not submit to God's law, nor can it do so. Those controlled by the sinful nature cannot please God. You, however, are controlled not by the sinful nature but by the Spirit, if the Spirit of God lives in you. And if anyone does not have the Spirit of Christ, he does not belong to Christ.

Every day you have the opportunity to feed either your sinful nature or the Spirit's involvement in your life. You can feed the "good dog," or you can feed the "bad dog." The dog that is fed the most is the one that will grow the strongest inside you and dominate your thought processes.

Living It Out

God has provided ample resources to help us in the battle to control our minds. By meditating on these verses, you will become more proficient at keeping the wrong content out and the good content in:

- "I will set before my eyes no vile thing. The deeds of faithless men I hate; they will not cling to me. Men of perverse heart shall be far from me; I will have nothing to do with evil" (Ps. 101:3-4).
- "How can a young man keep his way pure? By living according to your word. I seek you with all my heart; do not let me stray from your commands. I have hidden your word in my heart that I might not sin against you" (Ps. 119:9-11).
- "I urge you, brothers, in view of God's mercy, to offer your bodies as living sacrifices, holy and pleasing to God—this is your spiritual act of worship. Do not conform any longer to the pattern of this world, but be transformed by the renewing of your mind. Then you will be able to test and approve what God's will is—his good, pleasing and perfect will" (Rom. 12:1-2).
- "The peace of God, which transcends all understanding, will guard your hearts and your minds in Christ Jesus. Finally, brothers, whatever is true, whatever is noble, what-

ever is right, whatever is pure, whatever is lovely, whatever is admirable—if anything is excellent or praiseworthy—think about such things" (Phil. 4:7-8).

If you're really struggling with your thought life, choose one or two of the above passages to memorize and meditate on.

DAY SIXTEEN

Mind Motivation

Put me on trial, LORD, and cross-examine me. Test my motives and my heart. For I am always aware of your unfailing love, and I have lived according to your truth.

—Psalm 26:2-3, NLT

Reflection

It's easy for followers of Christ to put their faith on autopilot at times, isn't it? My ministry requires that I always be "on," so to speak. Sometimes I struggle with just going through the motions as opposed to doing what I do with a wholehearted focus on Jesus. Prayer is one of the main things that keep the focus of my passion on ministry, rather than simply going down an entertainment road. Each evening after dinner, my band and team all participate in a time of devotion and prayer. Then right before going onstage, we have a prayer huddle, and I think that helps set the tone by keeping our focus on Jesus.

Like Church

Sometimes I have to redirect my mind onstage to really think about the words as opposed to just singing a song I've sung a hundred times before. It is a very intentional discipline for me to say to myself, "Focus on what you're really communicating here!" If I feel that my heart isn't quite centered on God or I'm being distracted by something, I pray, "God, help me focus on You, and help me put aside the distractions."

Not too long ago I read a book by Larry Crabb titled, *The Pressure's Off.*[5] Dr. Crabb points out that we can do nothing to make God love us more or less—and that the goal of our lives needs to be God Himself, not His blessings. I think we've all been guilty of living for the wrong motivation, perhaps thinking thoughts like this: *Well, if I do this for God, if I go to church and serve Him and do the right things to live a holy life, then God will bless me!* We become motivated by the desire to be blessed with happiness, peace, and joy—living a life in which everything goes just right. Life doesn't always go exactly as we plan, and everything doesn't always go exactly as we'd like it to. But God promises to be there with us in the midst, despite the circumstances we are going through, whether good or bad.

God should be the ultimate goal in our lives. He is the reason we exist, and the Maker of every good thing that comes into our lives. We need to desire fellowship and intimacy with Him above all else. And when that happens, when He is our mind motivation, everything else falls into place.

Looking Further

The longest of the Psalms, 119, is a literary masterpiece. It is divided into twenty-two parts, according to the number of letters of the Hebrew alphabet, and each part consists of eight verses. Amazingly, all the verses of the first part begin with the first letter of the alphabet, *Aleph*; all the verses of the second part begin with *Beth*, the second letter of the alphabet; and so on, through the entire psalm. The psalm contains a number of thoughts that deal with keeping our minds focused on the proper motivation. The following are just the tip of the iceberg. . . .

✓ "I meditate on your precepts and consider your ways" (v. 15).

✓ "My soul is consumed with longing for your laws at all times" (v. 20).

✓ "Let me understand the teaching of your precepts; then I will meditate on your wonders" (v. 27).

✓ "I have considered my ways and have turned my steps to your statutes" (v. 59).

✓ "Oh, how I love your law! I meditate on it all day long" (v. 97).

✓ "I open my mouth and pant, longing for your commands" (v. 131).

Living It Out

How does your thinking motivate you? Take a few minutes today to read all 176 verses of Psalm 119 in one sitting. Then surrender your motivation for the day to God's desires for you. Take mental notes concerning what differences you observe in your day because of this prayer of submission.

DAY SEVENTEEN

Sweet Surrender

Don't put your confidence in powerful people; there is no help for you there.
When they breathe their last, they return to the earth, and all their plans die
with them. But joyful are those who have the God of Israel as their helper,
whose hope is in the LORD their God.

—Psalm 146:3-5, NLT

Reflection

A few years ago when I was asked to speak at the Bible Study Fellowship at the White House, I really didn't know what message to share. While flying home from another event the week before, I prayed that God would provide, and in that short flight I really felt Him give me the exact message I was meant to give. It was on spiritual warfare—particularly the spiritual warfare being faced by our leaders today. I felt as though I was supposed to talk about the "three D's"—*distraction, discouragement,* and *discontent*—areas in which we are coming under attack today.

When I shared this message that day in the White House, there was a definite sense of God's presence and His power being strong in my weakness. I came to God and said, "I really feel unqualified for this. I feel weak and overwhelmed. Speak through me and let me be Your mouthpiece." There was just such a beautiful atmosphere of God in that place. We worshipped together, we prayed, and then I shared the "three D's" message. I'll never forget the beautiful way God came through that day.

Just as I needed to rely on God that day, our quest for purity also begins by surrendering our minds and wills to our heavenly Father. We must be willing to pray a prayer of surrender, that we will choose to rely not on our own thoughts and abilities, but on Christ's alone. His thoughts are so much higher than our thoughts, and His ways than our ways! Our bodies cannot be pure if we have not first given our minds over to God. Jesus said in Mark 7:15, "Nothing outside a man can make him 'unclean' by going into him. Rather, it is what comes out of a man that makes him 'unclean.'" We have to be willing to give God all of our minds, to ask Him to remodel the inside—where our thoughts live. He loves it when we come to Him with this kind of sweet surrender.

God knows that anything else we put our trust in is going to let us down. The Lord is our comfort throughout all seasons of life. That is what gives me hope . . . for now and for the future. Everything else will change, but He is unchanging. This gives me enough confidence to give Him all of my trust, enough for me to say, "God, take all of me."

Looking Further

Sometimes it's easier for us to put our hope in things—such as people, relationships, possessions, or money—than in God. But God calls us to place all our hope in Him. Psalm 52:9 says, "I will praise you forever for what you have done; in your name I will hope, for your name is good." Isaiah 33:2-3 pleads, "GOD, treat us kindly. You're our only hope. First thing in the morning, be there for us! When things go bad, help us out! You spoke in thunder and everyone ran. You showed up and nations scattered" (THE MESSAGE). As we surrender more of ourselves to Him, we will recognize more and more of His goodness in our lives.

Living It Out

Confess to God the things in which you most often place your hope. Where does He rate on that list? Pray a simple prayer of surrender today and see what happens. Take Him at His word. He is enough.

DAY EIGHTEEN

Searching for Truth

This is GOD's Message, the God who made earth, made it livable and lasting, known everywhere as GOD: "Call to me and I will answer you. I'll tell you marvelous and wondrous things that you could never figure out on your own."
—Jeremiah 33:2-3, THE MESSAGE

Reflection

I'm not unlike many people who have grown up in the church. There's a lot about Christianity that we just accept from our parents. Too often it takes a dramatic moment of awakening for you to say, "I need to discover this for myself." A few years ago I came to a place in my life where I wanted to study more apologetics (the defense of the authenticity of God's truths and the claims of Christ). I wanted to be able to defend my faith in a greater way—not just for those who might not know Jesus and could challenge me, but also for myself. I really wanted to understand certain aspects of my faith that I hadn't looked at in depth before. I had unanswered questions about life, love, and what it means to trust God with all my heart.

I immersed myself in study, reading, and discussing my questions with a mentor and with an international community of others also on a search for truth. I processed what I learned, spent time in prayer, soul-searching, and serious in-depth Bible study, and listened for the still, small voice of God to speak. I was a sponge just taking it all in. It was a powerful season in my spiritual growth when faith and real life intersected.

I love the example of the Bereans in the New Testament. After hearing the apostle Paul speak, "they received the message with great eagerness and examined the Scriptures every day to see if what Paul said was true" (Acts 17:11). As a result, many of them accepted the claims of Jesus Christ and put their faith in Him. God doesn't want us to blindly accept whatever others say—whether parents, preachers, Bible teachers, or friends. He wants us to check out the validity of their words for ourselves. God is big enough to handle all of our questions, and if we will come to Him sincerely seeking His truth, He will answer.

Looking Further

Jesus' twelve apostles spent three years walking with Him and asking Him questions in an attempt to clarify in their own minds the meaning behind the words He spoke. Jesus said so many mind-boggling things that were diametrically opposed to much of what the disciples had been taught according to the Law. Sometimes Jesus spoke with figures of speech that they did not understand. Toward the end of His earthly ministry, they said, "Now we know that you know everything—it all comes together in you. You won't have to put up with our questions anymore. We're convinced you came from God" (John 16:30, THE MESSAGE).

After Jesus' resurrection, when He first appeared to His disciples, Thomas was not present (John 20:19-24). When the others told Thomas they had seen the Lord, he responded, "Unless I see the nail marks in his hands and put my finger where the nails were, and put my hand into his side, I will not believe it" (v. 25). He wanted physical proof of Christ's resurrection. A week later Jesus again appeared to them, and this time Thomas was in the room. After Jesus invited Thomas to touch Him, Thomas boldly exclaimed, "My Lord and my God!" (v. 28). When we come to God with our questions and He proves Himself to us in myriad ways, this is the most appropriate response—to follow His leading and lordship in our lives.

Living It Out

In your search for truth, are there certain things you believe about Christ that you have blindly accepted? Have you dug into God's Word to find the answers for yourself? If not, now is a good time to start. Are there others in your life who are seeking truth but don't know that they are really searching for a vibrant relationship with Jesus? What can you do to answer their questions in an honest way, and direct them to the ultimate Source of truth?

Carol Pierson

DAY NINETEEN

A Different Way of Thinking

Do not love this world nor the things it offers you, for when you love the world, you do not have the love of the Father in you. For the world offers only a craving for physical pleasure, a craving for everything we see, and pride in our achievements and possessions. These are not from the Father, but are from this world. And this world is fading away, along with everything that people crave. But anyone who does what pleases God will live forever.

—1 John 2:15-17, NLT

Reflection

It's so easy for us to buy into the current thinking of the day—whatever that is. Whether it concerns same-sex marriage, our politicians' views on abortion, the popular notion of a man and woman living together before marriage, or tolerating all world religions as equal in God's sight, Christians are often seen as intolerant if they don't swim with the current. God is concerned that we retain His views on these topics as He revealed them to us in His Word. He wants us to be pure in our thinking. Even though we must live in this world, God doesn't want us to allow the various strains of impurity to infect our hearts and minds. It's a high calling, but God intends for us to think radically different from the rest of the world.

People admire us when we stand for purity of life. They can see that we don't have to find love and acceptance and escape through doing drugs and drinking alcohol and engaging in promiscuous sex. When others see God's true love, joy, and peace lived out in practical ways, they will want what we have. We speak the loudest to non-Christians when we live out our faith. The Jesus difference is most noticeable in us when we not only talk about God but live our faith 24-7. That's our loudest witness. This should be our daily prayer: "God, show me how to live a life that's more pleasing to You."

Looking Further

We don't hear the word *holy* much in our culture today, unless it's used in a context in which someone is making fun of one who is a "holy roller" or has a "holier than thou" attitude. The root word means to be set apart or consecrated for a specific purpose. Here are some verses that should challenge our thinking:

✔ "We're being shown how to turn our backs on a godless, indulgent life, and how to take on a God-filled, God-honoring life. This new life is starting right now, and is whetting our appetites for the glorious day when our great God and Savior, Jesus Christ, appears. He offered himself as a sacrifice to free us from a dark, rebellious life into this good, pure life, making us a people he can be proud of, energetic in goodness" (Titus 2:12-14, THE MESSAGE).

✔ "You're cheating on God. If all you want is your own way, flirting with the world every chance you get, you end up enemies of God and his way. And do you suppose God doesn't care? The proverb has it that 'he's a fiercely jealous lover.' And what he gives in love is far better than anything else you'll find" (James 4:4-6, THE MESSAGE).

✔ "You must live as God's obedient children. Don't slip back into your old ways of living to satisfy your own desires. You didn't know any better then. But now you must be holy in everything you do, just as God who chose you is holy" (1 Pet. 1:14-15, NLT).

Living It Out

What prevents you from thinking and living differently from what you see all around you? In what specific ways would you like to be different from those around you? Make a list of those things, then talk to God about your desires and ask Him to empower you to walk a "set-apart" life today.

DAY TWENTY

Thinking Like a Child

Watch what God does, and then you do it, like children who learn proper behavior from their parents. Mostly what God does is love you. Keep company with him and learn a life of love. Observe how Christ loved us. His love was not cautious but extravagant. He didn't love in order to get something from us but to give everything of himself to us. Love like that.

—Ephesians 5:1-2, THE MESSAGE

Reflection

If I weren't involved in music as my primary avenue of ministry, I think I would be doing work with children in some capacity.

I've always had a heart for kids because they are so innocent and full of faith and wonder. When I was a child I dreamed of working in an orphanage and helping children in need. I've been able to fulfill part of that goal through child sponsorships with Compassion International. I also got to work with City of Hope, a children's relief network in Romania. I've witnessed firsthand what they are doing to minister to the kids who live under the streets in the sewers, and it's incredible! They are bringing the hope of our heavenly Father to kids who so desperately need it.

God longs to be our *Abba*, an Aramaic term that means "Daddy." He doesn't just want to be our formal Father, He wants to be our intimate Daddy! He desires for us to come to Him with open arms and reach up to Him in childlike faith and awe. Paul said, "All who are led by the Spirit of God are children of God. So you have not received a spirit that makes you fearful slaves. Instead, you received God's Spirit when he adopted you as his own children. Now we call him, 'Abba, Father.' For his Spirit joins with our spirit to affirm that we are God's children" (Rom. 8:14-16, NLT). He adds in Galatians that because God has bought our freedom, we now have "the full rights of sons." We can cry out "Abba, Father" because we are His heirs (Gal. 4:5-7).

Have you ever noticed how a little child sometimes imitates his dad's mannerisms, voice inflections, and actions? God desires that once we come to Him, we will imitate Him, loving the things He loves, hating the things He hates, giving to others the way He gives. As we get older we often lose our childlike innocence, our simple ways. Life often gets complicated, and because we are consumed with so many pursuits, we no longer approach life with the simple faith of children. God says, "Become like children once again and trust Me."

Looking Further

Jesus was never too busy to take time out to spend with children, talking with them and playing with them. The disciples shooed them off when they were brought to Jesus, but He intervened and said, "Let the children alone, don't prevent them from coming to me. God's kingdom is made up of people like these'" (Matt. 19:13-14, THE MESSAGE). Jesus affirmed the tremendous value of children.

After the apostles came to Jesus and asked Him, "Who is the greatest in the kingdom of heaven?" (Matt. 18:1), they got quite a wake-up call. Jesus called a small child over and put the child among them, and then He spoke these mind-blowing words that challenged their thinking:

> I tell you the truth, unless you turn from your sins and become like little children, you will never get into the Kingdom of Heaven. So anyone who becomes as humble as this little child is the greatest in the Kingdom of Heaven. And anyone who welcomes a little child like this on my behalf is welcoming me. But if you cause one of these little ones who trusts in me to fall into sin, it would be better for you to have a large millstone tied around your neck and be drowned in the depths of the sea. (Matt. 18:3-6, NLT)

Living It Out

Take a look at the children you see around you and learn from them. What does it mean for God to be your Abba, Father? Thank Him for adopting you into His family. Show Him that you trust Him by lifting up your arms to Him and asking for His provision for you today.

DAY TWENTY-ONE

Communal Thinking

I'm turning you over to God, our marvelous God whose gracious Word can make you into what he wants you to be and give you everything you could possibly need in this community of holy friends.

—Acts 20:32, THE MESSAGE

Reflection

Have you ever met someone who said, "I don't need the church. There are too many hypocrites in it. I can worship God in nature all by myself"? It is true that we can worship God on our own, but God created us to live in community. He knew just how much we would need one another. None of us have it completely together. We need safe places where we can share our joys and our struggles with others who can rejoice—and empathize—with us. When Jesus first sent His disciples out on a mission of goodwill, He sent them out in twos. They were able to encourage each other as they set out to spread the good news of His kingdom.

I have seen the body of Christ come together in a powerful way to reach people with the gospel. Record labels, radio stations, Christian television stations, newspaper and magazine staff, local promoters, church leadership, festival organizers, stage managers, agents, and band management all come together for a common goal—to reach as many people as possible with the message of Christ! When all these people work as a united team, great things happen. Together we can share the love of Christ more effectively than if we attempt to do so apart.

Perhaps at no other time is Christian unity demonstrated more powerfully than when there is a crisis. A few years ago when the tsunami hit Southeast Asia, the world rallied to provide real help for hurting people. As the hands and feet of Jesus, believers from around the globe came streaming into the countries that were devastated. God can bring good out of tragedy, and often His people are part of the solution. Many times when we look at a difficult situation and ask, "How could He ever bring any good out of that?" we come to see that His compassionate heart is expressed through the community of faith. We are one of the ways in which He brings comfort and peace. We really do need one another.

Looking Further

Out of necessity, the early church banded together to fight persecution and advance the cause of Christ. There was a spirit of unity that superseded individual agendas. Luke recorded these words:

> They committed themselves to the teaching of the apostles, the life together, the common meal, and the prayers. Everyone around was in awe—all those wonders and signs done through the apostles! And all the believers lived in

a wonderful harmony, holding everything in common. They sold whatever they owned and pooled their resources so that each person's need was met. (Acts 2:42-45, THE MESSAGE)

James, the Lord's brother, gives this practical advice about the importance of living at peace communally:

Real wisdom, God's wisdom, begins with a holy life and is characterized by getting along with others. It is gentle and reasonable, overflowing with mercy and blessings, not hot one day and cold the next, not two-faced. You can develop a healthy, robust community that lives right with God and enjoy its results *only* if you do the hard work of getting along with each other, treating each other with dignity and honor. (James 3:17-18, THE MESSAGE)

Living It Out

When you think about the community of faith closest to you, what is hardest about getting along with others? What aspects come easiest to you? Are there any situations you are aware of now in which you can be the hands and feet of Jesus?

Day Twenty-two

Do Your Possessions Possess You?

[Do] not be so preoccupied with getting, so you can respond to God's giving. People who don't know God and the way he works fuss over these things, but you know both God and how he works. Steep your life in God-reality, God-initiative, God-provisions. Don't worry about missing out. You'll find all your everyday human concerns will be met.

—Matthew 6:31-33, The Message

Reflection

Far too many people spend their lives in the continual pursuit of accumulating stuff. Whether they are on a quest for their dream home, the hottest car, or the most fashionable and highest priced clothes, they become so consumed with their desire for bigger and better that they make this their number one priority in life, and leave God out of the equation. In Jesus' parable of the sower and the soils in Matthew 13, He warned that this kind of pursuit of worldly riches and cares could take over our lives and choke out any possibility of bearing fruit for Him.

Among my favorite possessions are my cell phone and my computer, which I can't imagine being without. I am constantly texting friends while I'm on the road. A huge part of my world is caught up in my Mac because of iPhoto, iTunes, and e-mail. There are so many good memories held within my laptop. And when it comes to clothes, funky jackets are probably my guilty pleasure. But the things I would miss most if they were taken away from me are books. My Bible, Christian novels, and teaching books are incredibly important in my life. I want to constantly be growing, and these help ensure that I'm deepening my faith.

Possessions in and of themselves are not wrong. But if we are possessed by them, that's a problem. It all depends on the attitude we have concerning the things on which we spend our money and time. An attitude of greed is pervasive in our culture. We are continuously bombarded on TV and in magazines with ads telling us to amass more and more. We are often made to feel that we need the latest, the best, and the most expensive. We must constantly be on our guard to fight against a self-indulgent and materialistic attitude in our lives. Jesus calls us to seek Him and His kingdom first, then He'll take care of the rest.

Looking Further

Jesus had a lot to say about how we view our possessions. He knew how closely our hearts are tied to the things we own, as if we really own anything (see Ps. 24:1). For instance:

- "Don't store up treasures here on earth, where moths eat them and rust destroys them, and where thieves break in and steal. Store your treasures in heaven, where moths and rust cannot destroy, and thieves do not break in and steal. Wherever your treasure is, there the desires of your heart will also be" (Matt. 6:19-21, NLT).
- "You can't worship two gods at once. Loving one god, you'll end up hating the other. Adoration of one feeds contempt for the other. You can't worship God and Money both" (Matt. 6:24, THE MESSAGE).
- "Take care! Protect yourself against the least bit of greed.

Life is not defined by what you have, even when you have a lot" (Luke 12:15, THE MESSAGE).

A person is a fool to store up earthly wealth but not have a rich relationship with God" (Luke 12:21, NLT).

Living It Out

Are there any treasures you value today that may end up in tomorrow's trash? If an attitude of greed is something you struggle with, talk to God about it. How can you yield your possessions to His control? What will you do to demonstrate that serving Jesus is your top priority?

DAY TWENTY-THREE

A New Attitude

Since you have heard about Jesus and have learned the truth that comes from him, throw off your old sinful nature and your former way of life, which is corrupted by lust and deception. Instead, let the Spirit renew your thoughts and attitudes. Put on your new nature, created to be like God—truly righteous and holy.

—Ephesians 4:21-24, NLT

Reflection

One day I had a conversation with my brother Luke in the kitchen of our family's farmhouse. We both expressed our desire to grow closer to God and connect with Him deeply. We discussed how easy it is to fall into the trap of learning *about* God without really getting to know Him personally. We live in such an instant-information culture, with the ability to get on the Internet and discover all sorts of things about a favorite movie or sports star without ever having a personal relationship with that person. You may know tons *about* the person, but not really *know* the person.

Not just knowing about Him, but really *knowing* God is the key to living a pure life. None of us have lived out purity perfectly, and some of us have messed it up big-time. Whatever your past consists of, God can give you a new start. Whether you're married or single, when you go to Him, He can not only help you heal from the past but also send you into the future with new habits and a new determination to remain pure. It all starts with what you commit to in your mind.

In the Scripture verses on page 62, Paul told the Ephesians that they had "heard" and "learned" the truth about Jesus. But for there to be lasting change, they needed to allow God's Spirit to take up residence in their hearts and transform their "thoughts and attitudes" from the inside out. That's the way a new nature, created in the likeness of God, becomes apparent to others. Having this kind of purity of mind may require a lot of slow, diligent work, but it is well worth the end result—a life lived in confidence, free of fear and worry, knowing that God is pleased with your thoughts, attitudes, and motives.

Looking Further

One of the greatest examples in the Bible of someone who completely did a one-eighty from the inside out is the apostle John. He experienced a radical transformation in his thoughts and motives. When Jesus first called him and his brother James to follow Him, He named them *Boanerges*, which means "Sons of Thunder" (Mark 3:17). At one point in Jesus' ministry, He and His disciples passed through a Samaritan village, but the people there did not welcome Him. James and John asked Jesus if they should call down fire from heaven to destroy them. These rough fishermen were not exactly gentle guys filled with compassion.

But after walking with Jesus for three-plus years, John softened quite a bit and a completely new attitude took over in his life. He became known as the disciple whom Jesus loved. The Gospel of John and his three epistles are filled with multiple exhortations that we are to "love one another." John stands as a testimony to the truth of 2 Corinthians 5:17: "Anyone who belongs to Christ has become a new person. The old life is gone; a new life has begun!" (NLT)

Living It Out

Do you need a new attitude in any areas of your life? In what ways do you need God's Holy Spirit to do an extreme makeover in you from the inside out? Confess those aspects of your life to God today; then ask Him to effect change in your thoughts, motives, and habits.

DAY TWENTY-FOUR

The Center of His Will

Carefully build yourselves up in this most holy faith by praying in the Holy Spirit, staying right at the center of God's love, keeping your arms open and outstretched, ready for the mercy of our Master, Jesus Christ. This is the unending life, the real life!

—Jude 1:20-21, THE MESSAGE

Reflection

While sitting in my backyard a number of years ago, I wrote out my life mission statement. This is what I wrote: "I am a woman who loves God very much; He is my best friend and the center of my life. I want to share Him with everyone who will listen, whether through music, by giving my testimony before an audience, talking in one-on-one conversation, or through the way in which I live." I desire to be passionate about God and have everything else in my life flow from that passion. I have been given the opportunity through ministry to encourage families to live sold out for God, and to live His way. If He leads me somewhere else in the future, I'll willingly follow because my biggest goal in life is to be at the center of His will.

The sixth chapter of Galatians has been very helpful to me in thinking about my life's goal and my ministry. In verse 3 the apostle Paul says that we should not be impressed with ourselves. "If anyone thinks he is something when he is nothing, he deceives himself." One way to guard against thinking too much of yourself is to have major accountability in your life. My family has the biggest responsibility in keeping me accountable because they know me best and have always been honest with me. A huge priority for me is spending time with God in prayer and in the Bible. That certainly helps keep me from being too impressed with myself. I don't ever want to give others the impression that I think more of myself than I should. I just want to be someone who is real, down-to-earth, and serious about God.

In Galatians 6:4 we are admonished, "Each one should test his own actions . . . without comparing himself to somebody else." I think this means that we should not follow others' precedents, that we shouldn't do things just because "everyone else does it that way!" God desires that we be ourselves by being creative and fresh in our approach to life, rather than simply following the crowd. He wants us to depend on Him through prayer for everything we do (whether big or small), and not rush into things ahead of His will. When we seek His peace about a certain direction or life decision, He will answer and respond with what is best for us.

Looking Further

If we choose not to heed Paul's advice in Galatians 6, and think of ourselves as more important than we really are, there will be consequences. At some point in life, others may give us a reality check and tell us how it really is. Galatians 6:7-8 gives the final word on the outcome:

> Don't be misled—you cannot mock the justice of God. You will always harvest what you plant. Those who live only to satisfy their own sinful nature will harvest decay and death

from that sinful nature. But those who live to please the Spirit will harvest everlasting life from the Spirit. (NLT)

Living It Out

Have you ever written out a life mission statement? It really helps define who you want to be in the way that you interact with God and others. Carve out some time this week to talk to God about it, read His Word, and then write it out. A life mission statement can become a great tool by which you evaluate your decisions.

DAY TWENTY-FIVE

Overcoming Loneliness

May God himself, the God who makes everything holy and whole, make you holy and whole, put you together—spirit, soul, and body—and keep you fit for the coming of our Master, Jesus Christ. The One who called you is completely dependable. If he said it, he'll do it!

—1 Thessalonians 5:23-24, THE MESSAGE

Reflection

Loneliness. Not a fun word! Over the years I have often felt the toll of my continuous travel, especially in the area of romantic relationships. Ever felt that everyone around you is with someone . . . except you? I have.

Loneliness is a problem that plagues everyone, whether you're single or married. But God can really use the times of loneliness in our lives if we will let Him. We can be like Jesus and use the time to grow closer to God. Jesus often went off by Himself to be alone with His Father in prayer (see Luke 5:16). When we're alone with God, without the distractions of the world, we can hear His voice much more clearly. Then we can seek to do His will.

Amen

The apostle Peter challenges us with these words: "Be generous with the different things God gave you, passing them around so all get in on it: if words, let it be God's words; if help, let it be God's hearty help. That way, God's bright presence will be evident in everything through Jesus, and he'll get all the credit as the One mighty in everything" (1 Pet. 4:10-11, THE MESSAGE). Even when we're feeling lonely, God calls us to give ourselves away by serving others. Every day we see so many people who are hurting and need us to share Jesus' love with them. Can you imagine what would happen if every Christ follower took that responsibility to love seriously? Revival would break out.

When you are walking in intimacy with God, one is a whole number. He promises to meet all your emotional and social needs, and He is dependable to do it. It becomes a matter of changing our minds and attitudes from feeling sorry for ourselves to being grateful we have time to spend alone with God and to reach out in service to others in need of companionship and care.

Looking Further

Abraham was a hundred years old, and his wife, Sarah, was ninety when God answered their prayers and gave them the son of promise, Isaac (see Gen. 21). Then God asked Abraham to do the unthinkable: to sacrifice his son as a burnt offering as a test of his faith, and in obedience Abraham complied. He bound his son, and just as he was about to plunge the knife into him, an angel of the Lord stopped him. He had passed the test. Abraham looked up and saw a ram caught by its horns in the thicket nearby. God had provided the necessary sacrifice, so Abraham renamed Mount Moriah, where this took place, *Jehovah-jireh*, "The LORD Will Provide" (Gen. 22:14).

This name for God combines the covenant name by which God was known (derived from *havah*, "to be") with the Hebrew word *yireh*, which means "to look upon," "to see," "to provide."[6] We might translate it this way: "Jehovah will see to it," or "Jehovah's provision shall be seen." Just as God looked upon Abraham's plight and responded, He sees and provides for all our needs . . . even loneliness.

Living It Out

There are people in your life—at home, at school, at work, in your neighborhood—who would love to know that someone else cares about them. God is still *Jehovah-jireh*, and He loves to provide for our needs. The next time you feel lonely, think about the people you could minister to. Identify practical ways you can serve them in God's name. When you reach out to others, you will be encouraged and God will be pleased.

DAY TWENTY-SIX

Daring to Dream

God can do anything, you know—far more than you could ever imagine or guess or request in your wildest dreams! He does it not by pushing us around but by working within us, his Spirit deeply and gently within us.

—Ephesians 3:20, THE MESSAGE

Reflection

This past year I've been involved in a study group that includes three other people, all involved in music and ministry. We call ourselves the "Soul Check Society" because our main purpose is to help our members go deeper in community with God and one another. Each month we read a book and write an essay on it or have a question that we respond to via e-mail, since we live in three different cities. We take turns deciding which book to read and what questions we will answer. It's been a very enriching experience. One of our questions was this: "Do you have any unrealized dreams? If you could picture your life in its most fulfilled state, one in which you are absolutely alive to all the possibilities God has placed in your heart, what would that look like?"

A friend of my family led devotions before one of our concerts. He said that as people grow up most of them forget to dream, or simply don't take time for it. I think that many of us, myself included, are scared to dream because dreaming potentially invites disappointment if those desires go unfulfilled.

No!

On the other hand, *not* being willing to dream keeps us out of touch with certain parts of our hearts, and therefore we live but are not fully *alive*. I don't want to live that way anymore. I want my heart to be fully alive and kicking—even if it does hurt at times.

Here are some of my unrealized dreams:

- To be married, have a family, and be a strong support to my husband in his calling.
- To write a song that lives in the church beyond my lifetime and calls people to an intimate worship experience with God.
- To act in a film suitable for family viewing, preferably a period piece that is quality production (both in content and in technical excellence).
- To come to a place of balance in life.
- To have such an intimate walk with God and receive His love in such a powerful way that all my life is strengthened with joy and peace no matter the trials I might be walking through. Amen.

Looking Further

God doesn't want us to settle for mediocrity in our lives. He doesn't want us to just grow old and let go of our dreams. He spoke through the prophet Joel when He said, "I will pour out my Spirit on all people. Your sons and daughters will prophesy, your old men will dream dreams, your young men will see visions" (Joel 2:28). Peter quoted this passage on the Day of Pentecost after the Holy Spirit came in a powerful way. Through the pages of the Bible, God often revealed His will in dreams and visions. He worked mightily in the lives of

Joseph and Daniel in giving them the gift of the interpretation of dreams. (See Gen. 37, 40–41; Dan. 2, 4–5, 7.) We have a God who loves fulfilling big dreams.

Solomon said, "Much dreaming and many words are meaningless. Therefore stand in awe of God" (Eccl. 5:7). Our dreams, apart from God, mean nothing. But when we lay our dreams before Him and submit them to His will, He accomplishes more than we ever dreamed or imagined. He says to us today: "Risk your life and get more than you ever dreamed of. Play it safe and end up holding the bag" (Luke 19:26, THE MESSAGE). The choice is up to us.

Living It Out

What unrealized dreams do you have? If you could picture your life in its most fulfilled state, one in which you are absolutely alive to all the possibilities God has placed in your heart, what would that look like? Spend some time today talking to God about that; then compose a list of dreams God has placed in your heart.

DAY TWENTY-SEVEN

Dreaming of Heaven

Because Jesus was raised from the dead, we've been given a brand-new life and have everything to live for, including a future in heaven—and the future starts now! God is keeping careful watch over us and the future. The Day is coming when you'll have it all—life healed and whole.

—1 Peter 1:3-5, THE MESSAGE

Reflection

My Soul Check Society also answered the question: "How do you view heaven and hell? And how does this perspective impact your daily life?" I have a hard time picturing hell and don't really spend much time dwelling on it. The thought of people being damned, existing in agony forever, is very troubling to me. I have in mind a loose picture of pitch-black darkness, loneliness, utter sadness, and stifling heat. I think if I had a better grasp on what hell is really like it would definitely increase my passion to see more people saved.

I view heaven as a place where finally no veil, or cloud, hangs between God and me. Sometimes I long to see Him so much that I actually reach my hand out as if to touch His face. I long to see Him clearly and sometimes get frustrated because it feels like I can't. I imagine Jesus and me seeing each other for the first time face-to-face in heaven, with recognition in our eyes and smiles lighting our faces. Then I'm held by Him. I picture heaven consisting of fields of flowers with mountains and lakes

[handwritten margin note:] If it is troubling to you, might it also belong to troubling to God?

surrounding them. Because nothing is holding me back anymore in this heavenly environment, I can run and dance and play with utter abandon.

I most look forward to being with Jesus for all eternity because the race will have been won and we won't have to struggle to the point of exhaustion anymore. But even as I dream of heaven, I love the thought that we can begin to live heaven now. Maybe it's a God-consciousness that allows us to live with a sense of peace and security despite our present circumstances. Perhaps it's constantly being aware that this world is not our home and we ache for the perfection of heaven. Dreaming about heaven now and again can help us get through the challenges of our daily lives.

Looking Further

Revelation chapters 21 and 22 give us a glimpse into how incredibly beautiful heaven will be. The description found there cannot begin to compare with the reality of its splendor. The apostle Paul said:

> We know that when these bodies of ours are taken down like tents and folded away, they will be replaced by resurrection bodies in heaven. . . . Sometimes we can hardly wait to move—and so we cry out in frustration. Compared to what's coming, living conditions around here seem like a stopover in an unfurnished shack, and we're tired of it! We've been given a glimpse of the real thing, our true home, our resurrection bodies! The Spirit of God whets our appetite by giving us a taste of what's ahead. He puts a little of heaven in our hearts so that we'll never settle for less. (2 Cor. 5:1-5, THE MESSAGE)

Does he eventually come to struggle to the point of exhaustion now?

And so we might give of heaven to others so that they might yearn for it as well.

According to Paul, this is one of the things that keep us going. He says in Colossian 3:1-4:

> Since you have been raised to new life with Christ, set your sights on the realities of heaven, where Christ sits in the place of honor at God's right hand. Think about the things of heaven, not the things of earth. For you died to this life, and your real life is hidden with Christ in God. And when Christ, who is your life, is revealed to the whole world, you will share in all his glory. (NLT)

Living It Out

As you dream of heaven today, read Revelation 21–22, and then close your eyes and try to imagine being there with Jesus for all eternity. What images come to your mind? How can those images motivate you to walk in purity today?

DAY TWENTY-EIGHT

A Thankful Attitude

Thank you! Everything in me says "Thank you!" Angels listen as I sing my thanks. I kneel in worship facing your holy temple and say it again: "Thank you!" Thank you for your love, thank you for your faithfulness; most holy is your name, most holy is your Word. The moment I called out, you stepped in; you made my life large with strength.

—Psalm 138:1-3, THE MESSAGE

Reflection

Our lives can easily get too complex. Too busy. Too full. Too complicated. Every now and then we need to get off the train of activity, slow down, and pause to think about all the amazing blessings God brings into our lives every day. It's easy to coast through life until we have a reality check and see just how much we have been given. These moments of realization, of gratitude, are my most intense times of worship. Times when I really thank God and deeply praise Him.

I love the simplicity of the song "Thank You." Whether we're consumed with our busyness in the good times or trying to see our way through the tough times, we need to be reminded of the truth of the lyric:

Something I know is amiss in my soul.
My eyes are on me.
This should not be.
I'll praise you from the center of my fire.[7]

We tend to get in trouble when we spend too much time with our eyes focused on ourselves rather than dwelling on the things that most please God. You might be going through the "center of the fire" right now, or you may feel as though you are on top of the world. Either way, we are admonished to give thanks in all things (see I Thess. 5:18). Being thankful to God should help motivate us to live lives of purity before Him. It is because of all that He has done for us that we want to please Him with our attitudes, words, and actions.

Looking Further

Psalm 136 is a great psalm to meditate on when the theme for the day is thanksgiving. In these twenty-six verses, the psalmist itemizes all the good things God has done for which he is grateful: God's goodness; His sovereignty over all; His great wonders; His creation of heaven and earth, the sun and the moon; His deliverance of His people from Egypt; His victories in the Promised Land; and the freedom He offers to His people. He realizes that God's people are to be in a continual attitude of thanksgiving.

We are admonished in Colossians 3:17: "Let every detail in your lives—words, actions, whatever—be done in the name of the Master, Jesus, thanking God the Father every step of the way" (THE MESSAGE). And again in Hebrews 13:15: "Let us offer through Jesus a continual sacrifice of praise to God, proclaiming our allegiance to his name" (NLT). It's an attitude that we must work at cultivating.

Living It Out

When was the last time you listed on a piece of paper all the things for which you are thankful? Think of the huge blessings in your life as well as the little ones, the ones you often take for granted (like clean drinking water and shelter), and also those you thank God for every day. Write them all down. Then place the list inside your Bible. The next time you are going through the "center of the fire," pull the list out and give thanks to God again for the blessings in your circumstances.

DAY TWENTY-NINE

The Shadowlands

My aim is to raise hopes by pointing the way to life without end. This is the life God promised long ago—and he doesn't break promises!

—Titus 1:2, THE MESSAGE

Reflection

Since I was a child, I've been inspired by the writings of C. S. Lewis. He wrote about the "shadowlands" as a symbol for his struggle with personal pain and grief. He talked about enduring suffering with patience, then living it out as his beloved wife, Joy, became afflicted with cancer and eventually died. To me the shadowlands represent the times in our lives when we feel like we are walking through a valley filled with a deep cloud—and we just don't see how we're going to move out of it. In those seasons we lose hope and can't see the light at the end of the journey. Some authors have referred to this experience as "the dark night of the soul."

I've been in those spots before in my own life—times when feelings of discouragement and vulnerability surrounded me. I wrote the song "Shadowlands" not only to describe the reality of this situation but also to offer hope in the midst of it. There is hope in God, who is constantly there with us even in the shadowlands. He will bring us through, out of the clouds and back into the light. We must focus our minds on this hope while we are in the valley. My favorite part of the song is the bridge, where it says:

I know it's true,
all that you say.
I believe in you
and I am standing on
the promises you've made.
You promised me and I believe.[8]

Out of the shadowlands, Job spoke this truth: "He uncovers mysteries hidden in darkness; he brings light to the deepest gloom" (Job 12:22, NLT). David said, "Even when the way goes through Death Valley, I'm not afraid when you walk at my side. Your trusty shepherd's crook makes me feel secure" (Ps. 23:4, THE MESSAGE). The prophet Isaiah foretold a time coming when the Messiah would deliver God's people from the shadowlands: "The people walking in darkness have seen a great light; on those living in the land of the shadow of death a light has dawned" (Isa. 9:2).

Looking Further

Second Peter 1:4 says that God has given us His "very great and precious promises" so that we can participate in the exciting life that He offers and overcome the world's corruption. Here are some of His awesome promises we can cling to while in the shadowlands:

- He will never leave us or forsake us (see Deut. 31:6; Heb. 13:5).
- He won't let us be tempted beyond what we can handle (see 1 Cor. 10:13).
- If we sow in tears, we'll reap in joy (see Ps. 126:5-6).
- When we cry out to Him, He hears and will save us (see Ps. 145:19).
- If we draw near to Him, He will draw near to us (see James 4:8).
- If we humble ourselves, He will lift us up (see James 4:10).
- If we are in need of rest, He will provide it (see Matt. 11:28).
- If we need strength to resist the evil one, He will supply it (see 2 Thess. 3:3).

Living It Out

Which of God's promises listed above do you need to memorize and meditate on today? His promises will always be true. It is impossible for God to lie. Take Him at His word at all times, and especially if you are in the shadowlands.

DAY THIRTY

Help Us Remember

God, with undeserved kindness, declares that we are righteous. He did this through Christ Jesus when he freed us from the penalty for our sins. For God presented Jesus as the sacrifice for sin. People are made right with God when they believe that Jesus sacrificed his life, shedding his blood.

—Romans 3:24-25, NLT

Reflection

Like the hard drive on a computer, our brains have an unbelievable capacity for remembering specific experiences. And the things that we remember have the power to either free us or keep us in bondage. One of the things that really help purify my mind is meditating on what Jesus accomplished for me on the cross. When I first viewed *The Passion of the Christ*, I wept and empathized with Jesus like never before. It was definitely the most faith-deepening film I have ever seen. I now understand what Jesus went through for me almost as if I had been there. I truly believe that film was used as an instrument of God to reach out to Christians and non-Christians alike.

The most gripping scene for me was when Jesus had just stumbled underneath the weight of the cross. His mother, Mary, rushed to reach out to Him, and the film flashed back to a time when Jesus was a little boy and fell—we saw her running to Him then too. I wept at that point, as it was such a powerful scene. Jesus turned to her in the midst of His pain and said,

"Mother, see, I make all things new." I loved the power in those words and the realization that that's indeed what He came to do—to make all things new for all of us, to breathe life into us and give us new hope.

I ministered at a youth conference where Mel Gibson made a guest appearance to give a preview of the movie. In the process of speaking, he told a story that touched me quite deeply. The story was about a nun who had recently viewed his film. So moved was she that she prayed, "Jesus, I'm sorry. . . . I forgot." No matter how many Good Fridays and Sundays we hear the story of the death of Jesus on a Roman cross, may we never forget the gruesome reality of the sacrifice Jesus made for us. When it gets tough to maintain a pure mind in the midst of an impure generation, remembering Jesus' death can motivate us to not give up.

Looking Further

Every time you commune with Jesus by remembering His body broken and blood shed for you, you have the opportunity to make all things new. No matter what transgressions you've committed, there is forgiveness because of your right standing with God through the sacrifice of His Son. Without the shedding of blood, there is no forgiveness for sin (see Heb. 9:22), but because of Jesus we have these benefits:

> We can boldly enter heaven's Most Holy Place because of the blood of Jesus. By his death, Jesus opened a new and life-giving way through the curtain into the Most Holy Place. And since we have a great High Priest who rules over God's house, let us go right into the presence of God

with sincere hearts fully trusting him. For our guilty consciences have been sprinkled with Christ's blood to make us clean, and our bodies have been washed with pure water. (Heb. 10:19-22, NLT)

Living It Out

Make time today to remember some of the details of Christ's crucifixion by reading John 19. Thank Him for His extreme sacrifice for you, confess any known sin in your life, and praise Him for the gift of forgiveness.

PURITY OF BODY

Day Thirty-one

Waiting for Sex

Just because something is technically legal doesn't mean that it's spiritually appropriate. If I went around doing whatever I thought I could get by with, I'd be a slave to my whims. You know the old saying, "First you eat to live, and then you live to eat"? Well, it may be true that the body is only a temporary thing, but that's no excuse for stuffing your body with food, or indulging it with sex. Since the Master honors you with a body, honor him with your body!
— 1 Corinthians 6:12-13, The Message

Reflection

It all started when I was fifteen years old and attended a True Love Waits rally where I made a public commitment to save sex for marriage. I started performing at True Love Waits rallies, and the organizers asked me to share my commitment to save sex for marriage. Parents and teens alike thanked me for taking this public stance. Since that time, I've encouraged many young women to stick with their convictions about purity. You too *can* obey God's call for purity in your life.

In addition to setting some strong physical boundaries and dressing modestly, another key to maintaining my sexual purity is praying with and for the guys I've dated. I think the more we focus on God and pray about the relationship, the less likely we are to succumb to sexual temptation.

Some songs take months or even years to write, but "Wait for Me" came miraculously in about thirty or forty minutes. I had been praying that God would provide a song that I could sing about purity. In more than thirteen years of ministry, "Wait for Me" has connected with more people than anything else I've ever written. I know I represent young women all over the world who have been liberated from the pressure to conform to the "if it feels good, just do it" mentality that is so prevalent. The song was a gift to me from God. It's been a delight to receive thousands of e-mails, communications, and letters from people all over the globe who have been impacted by its message.

Waiting until marriage for sex is becoming a new benchmark of coolness—not only in the United States, but also throughout much of Western culture. Some churches still sponsor a yearly rally or event stressing their commitment to purity. Perhaps you've had the opportunity to attend an event of this nature. I hope you agree with me that abstinence is the smart way to go. We want to avoid consequences like STDs, AIDS, and pregnancy outside marriage; and besides all that, sexual abstinence before marriage really is God's way!

Looking Further

The greatest building in the city of Corinth was the temple of Aphrodite, the goddess of erotic love, where idolatry and immorality were rampant. Because the Christians in that city lived in such a totally sex-saturated society, the apostle Paul had some strong words to pass on to the believers there:

- "Run from sexual sin! No other sin so clearly affects the body as this one does. For sexual immorality is a sin against your own body" (1 Cor. 6:18, NLT).
- "The wife's body does not belong to her alone but also to

her husband. In the same way, the husband's body does not belong to him alone but also to his wife" (1 Cor. 7:4).

Living It Out

We live in a sex-saturated society today as well. It seems as if it's everywhere . . . in pop music, on TV, in the movies, on the Internet, in government, and in our schools. But God's words of love and protection for us are still true. He asks us to save sex for marriage because He knows what is best for us. Do you need to talk with Him about this issue, repent of a specific sin, or tell Him of your desire to obey Him in this area? Whatever your thoughts, He knows already, and He is eager for you to approach Him openly and honestly.

DAY THIRTY-TWO

Looking for Love

Jesus made a circuit of all the towns and villages. He taught in their meeting places, reported kingdom news, and healed their diseased bodies, healed their bruised and hurt lives. When he looked out over the crowds, his heart broke. So confused and aimless they were, like sheep with no shepherd.

—Matthew 9:35-36, THE MESSAGE

Reflection

All of us are in desperate need of love. Unfortunately, a lot of teenage girls and young women that I meet are looking for love in the wrong places. They look for it in a guy's physical attention and affection—and too often the attention they get comes from dressing immodestly and performing sexually. Some young women struggle with taking drugs, cutting themselves, and other various addictions, which usually stem from the hopelessness they face because of a lack of feeling deeply loved. The end results include extraordinarily low self-esteem, teen pregnancies, diseases, and even suicide. I sincerely hope your situation is not this desperate. I want you to know that there is hope!

Some of the angst and hopelessness I've seen among young people today arises from the genuine loss of reasons to live. Perhaps they've never really felt accepted—at home or among their peers. One big problem with many people is that they surround themselves with peers who are searching just as desperately as they are. When we hang around people who are speaking negative things into our lives, it's tough to feel hopeful ourselves.

You might be asking yourself, *Where is God in all of this?* God is passionate about His love for you. Everything else in the Christian life flows from that. We can get into a very legalistic place where faith just becomes religion, but the essence of the Christian life needs to be lived out from the knowledge of God's extravagant love. Once we understand and accept His love, so many other things in our lives fall into place. Things start to make sense. (I can't imagine going through life without realizing how incredible God's love is for me. I don't know how people make it without this knowledge.) This is the hope, truth, and life this generation is looking for—and all these things are found in Jesus!

Looking Further

The cure for the hopelessness that exists in the lives of so many people today is radical hope, which is recorded all over the pages of the Bible. In the Psalms, David often proclaimed to God that he had put his hope in Him alone (25:5, 21; 39:7; 62:5). The Weeping Prophet, Jeremiah, knew that it was only in the hope of the Lord that Israel would rise from the ashes (Jer. 14:22; 29:11; 31:17; Lam. 3:21-24).

The Apostle of Love, John, summed it all up so well:

How great is the love the Father has lavished on us, that we should be called children of God! And that is what we are! The reason the world does not know us is that it did not know him. Dear friends, now we are children of God, and what we will be has not yet been made known. But we know that when he appears, we shall be like him, for we shall see him as he is. Everyone who has this hope in him purifies himself, just as he is pure. (1 John 3:1-3)

We should live in such a way that others see our actions and attitudes and want what we have. The apostle Peter gives this challenge, "In your hearts set apart Christ as Lord. Always be prepared to give an answer to everyone who asks you to give the reason for the hope that you have. But do this with gentleness and respect" (1 Pet. 3:15).

Living It Out

Do you know someone who is in desperate need of hope and love? Is there something simple you can do today to communicate God's love in a practical way? What about composing and sending a thoughtful letter or e-mail, serving the person in secret (by dropping off a surprise gift in her mailbox, or having flowers or a pizza delivered), or some other kind of thoughtful gesture? Then pray for God's love to break through the hopelessness that you sense.

How I do for want this do this my students

DAY THIRTY-THREE

You Are Loved

When he was still a long way off, his father saw him. His heart pounding, he ran out, embraced him, and kissed him.

—Luke 15:20, THE MESSAGE

Reflection

I was thinking about what I wanted to write for a new album a few years ago. A childhood friend from Sydney, Australia, who I knew had fallen away from God, very randomly came to mind—and I felt that this "random" thought was actually placed there by God. I asked myself, *If I had one chance to tell Daniel something, what would I say to him?* The message I felt God really laid on my heart was to tell him, "You are loved." This became the title of a song on the album *If I Had One Chance to Tell You Something.* It is a song for the prodigals—which is what we all are. God is the Father who has His arms open wide waiting for us. He wants us to run toward Him, and He will run to welcome us.

From this song came the album title—and really the key theme of the project. I've come to realize that we need to stand in awe of God and be blown away by His power. But it's really His kindness and His love that draw us to Him and into a relationship with Him. His love makes us desire to know Him and love Him in return. That is the most important message I need to share through my life. From how I relate in my relationships with others to what I say onstage, the message is: "We are extravagantly loved by God."

It's a message of hope we all need to hear. No matter where you've been and what you've done . . . you are loved. In your battle for purity, one of the ongoing messages the enemy will throw at you is this line: "You've messed up; therefore, you are not worthy of being loved." If he can get you to believe that, he can get you to give up and lower your standards for purity. Please do not believe this lie from the pit of hell. You are loved!

Looking Further

Although most people think of the narrative Jesus told in Luke 15 as the parable of the prodigal son, in reality it is the story of the "loving father," because the lesson to be learned is more about the father's incredible love than the son's rebellion. Most everyone you know at one time or another has played the part of the prodigal. They either have run away from God through willful, deliberate sin for a relatively short season of time, or have left the fold and sought to live their own way for an extended period. When that happens, what's the appropriate response? Much has been written about the necessity for tough love from parents and friends toward one who has willingly turned aside to wallow in the mire of a pigs' sty. But even though the father in this story allowed his son his freedom (and even gave him his inheritance), he never stopped looking and waiting for his return home. And his message would always be, "You are loved."

Living It Out

Is there someone in your life who needs to know he is loved? Do you have a friend who is broken and desperately needs to know that she is loved? Our Abba Father's love for all of His creation is far beyond anything we can possibly imagine. Pray for an opportunity to speak God's words of love to the one who desperately needs to know; then, when God provides the open door for you, walk through it in obedience.

DAY THIRTY-FOUR

Safe, Healthy, and Empowered

Guide older women into lives of reverence so they end up as neither gossips nor drunks, but models of goodness. By looking at them, the younger women will know how to love their husbands and children, be virtuous and pure, keep a good house, be good wives. We don't want anyone looking down on God's Message because of their behavior.

—Titus 2:3-5, THE MESSAGE

Reflection

Have you ever felt overwhelmed? I have. Do you know what your role is supposed to be? Are you concerned that you don't measure up to other women? Me too. Maybe you're facing pressures at home and school and work because of all the different hats of responsibility you have to wear. On top of that, because of the outer beauty you see valued in today's culture, you may feel as if you are supposed to look like a model and be superskinny in order to be accepted. I conducted a survey on my Web site a few years ago, and more than a thousand women responded. The subject most talked about (by 75 percent of the respondents) had to do with appearance. The media's pressure to look a certain way is unbelievable, and talk of purity is virtually nonexistent.

In the book entitled *SHE: Safe, Healthy, and Empowered*, a co-author and I addressed many of the issues facing young women today.[9] The book struck such a nerve with people that it evolved into an event that we host from time to time in churches across America. The unique face of *SHE* is that it is a cross-generational women's event, with an audience filled with the responsive faces of "girls from eight to eighty." We discovered that women are hungry to talk about such topics as sexual purity, intimacy with God and others, holistic beauty, boundaries, mentoring, and purpose in life. God desires that we continue to grow in the truths He would have us believe about ourselves rather than taking our cues from the world.

Looking Further

In contrast to the majority of men in His day, who treated women as property, Jesus placed a high value on the worth of women. He treated all women with respect, from His earthly mother, Mary, to those ostracized by society. Think about the way He interacted with the outcast woman at the well (see John 4) and the woman caught in adultery (see John 8). He saw them not for what they once were, not as objects to be scorned, but for what they could become—women forgiven for their past and looking forward to a bright future. He met women at their point of need. No woman was ever beyond the reach of Jesus' mercy and grace. Because of the way He affirmed their worth, is it any wonder that women followed Jesus with such devotion, sat at the foot of the cross, accompanied His body to the tomb, and were the first to arrive at the burial place on the morning of His resurrection?

Living It Out

What does God desire for you as His daughter? If He were to speak to you today, what do you think He would say regarding your inner beauty, your desire for holiness and purity? What words of affirmation would He speak about your talents and gifts and how you could use them in an even greater way for Him? Imagine that He desires to speak these truths into your life today, then go and meet with Him.

DAY THIRTY-FIVE

Pure Speech

Though some tongues just love the taste of gossip, Christians have better uses for language than that. Don't talk dirty or silly. That kind of talk doesn't fit our style. Thanksgiving is our dialect.

—Ephesians 5:4, THE MESSAGE

Reflection

Not too long ago, I got to go to Chicago and record the voice of an animated character for a VeggieTales release entitled *An Easter Carol*. It was a very fun experience. When they found out I had done this, my friends teased me about being "Suzie Squash." I set the record straight and told them that I was actually an angel named Hope. Now it's quite amusing when little children come up to me and ask me to do the voice of Hope.

Exploring the dramatic side with my speaking voice is something that's very much in my family. My grandmother taught elocution (the art of effective public speaking) and did dramatic speech work when she was my age. It's been pretty cool to have her mantle passed on to me in this kind of work. I'm honored to receive the baton from her and carry the flame. Currently, I am in training with an acting coach, who is teaching me to have a standard American accent, so that as acting opportunities arise, I can swap over and get rid of my Australian accent, like Nicole Kidman, Russell Crowe, and other Aussies do. I've always been a bit of a mimic. As I progress further into the training, there are some word endings that are a real challenge to me—but I am definitely enjoying the process!

Our everyday speech betrays what's in our hearts and minds. The words that come from our lips are not some kind of role we are playing. Our words represent who we are. When people think of us, they often think of favorite things we say, or the way we word particular phrases. A true mark of a radical believer is that she is striving to possess purity of speech. But *unlike* acting, pure speech should be real, authentic, and grounded in a pure heart and mind.

Looking Further

The word *purity* is often used to describe something that is free from dust, dirt, or taintedness (as in *pure* springwater). When we drink bottled water, we expect it to be free of impurities. No one in his right mind would purposely sell impure water.

The words that we speak should not give mixed messages to others, but only messages that are consistent with who we say we are—followers of Christ. James, the brother of Jesus, had this to say:

> This is scary: You can tame a tiger, but you can't tame a tongue—it's never been done. The tongue runs wild, a wanton killer. With our tongues we bless God our Father; with the same tongues we curse the very men and women he made in his image. Curses and blessings out of the same mouth!
>
> My friends, this can't go on. A spring doesn't gush fresh water one day and brackish the next, does it? Apple trees don't bear strawberries, do they? Raspberry bushes don't bear apples, do they? You're not going to dip into a polluted mud hole and get a cup of clear, cool water, are you? (James 3:7-12, THE MESSAGE)

Living It Out

Paul told Timothy, "Don't let anyone think less of you because you are young. Be an example to all believers in what you say, in the way you live, in your love, your faith, and your purity" (1 Tim. 4:12, NLT). How pure is your everyday speech? Are there some things that need to change? Talk with God about your desire to improve in this area, and then trust Him to help you.

DAY THIRTY-SIX

🦋

Humble and Pure of Heart

God blesses those whose hearts are pure, for they will see God.

—Matthew 5:8, NLT

Reflection

My travels overseas have always been filled with wonderful experiences, perhaps none more delightful than our trip to Oberhofen, Austria, set in the shadows of the towering peaks of the Alps. The little town has a population of sixteen hundred, and most of the folks there had never been to a contemporary concert, let alone heard of contemporary Christian music. Our extraordinary day began at 8:00 a.m. on a cold, clear morning in January, when a young choir enthusiastically greeted our tour bus. On this particular stint through Europe (six concerts in seven days), we had many late nights and early mornings, so most of us didn't emerge that morning until noon. The choir sang lovely local music, the mayor welcomed us, and the local Catholic priest, Christoph Haider (who had also taken care of many of the details of the concert), prayed over our meal before opening the rather large rectory for us to enjoy.

Mid-afternoon, while sound equipment was being set up, the priest and his interpreter took us for a walk around the village. We were surrounded on every side by huge beautiful mountain peaks. The priest, whom we affectionately called "Father," explained how he had discovered our ministry and why we were there. A year prior to our visit, he realized he needed to communicate the gospel to his young people in a more relevant way. He stumbled onto my music via the Internet. He knew of my passionate message of abstinence before marriage and felt that was the message the village needed to hear.

He shared that the young people in the village, including those in his church choir, were living together as young as sixteen years of age. Believe it or not, this was happening with the support of their parents. "Father" told us that he often felt hopeless when parents reasoned that it was a new day and the times had changed. The kids had adopted the values of TV celebrities and mainstream rock stars, totally unaware that there was a better way of living available to them. The concept of sexual abstinence wasn't even a consideration.

That evening at our concert, we were given a tremendous opportunity to present a new way of living and a challenge to go deeper into the Christian life. After the altar call, most of the six hundred present prayed a prayer of commitment. Even though that was the smallest concert of this leg, everyone on the road felt that we had been somehow changed as well. We had witnessed the extraordinary servanthood of a rural priest who faithfully loved his congregation regardless of their response. That is purity of heart. It was a defining moment in all our lives. We fell in love with Father's ministry in that place so much that we decided to return—and did so a year later.

Looking Further

In your quest for physical purity, your attitude should be the same as that of the priest of Oberhofen. He was humble and faithful in the midst of many around him who were living only for self. When you think of the *perfect* model for purity of heart, you have to think of Jesus. He is humble and gentle of heart, and He exemplified this by giving up His divine privileges to take on the form of a human being. He spent His whole life serving others and meeting their needs ahead of His own. Jesus washed the dirty feet of His apostles on the eve of His betrayal, then in humility submitted Himself in obedience to God and died a criminal's death on a cross. That's a purity that goes beyond physical purity—it's a radical purity of heart that affects all of life.

The apostle Paul challenged us: "Run from anything that stimulates youthful lusts. Instead, pursue righteous living, faithfulness, love, and peace. Enjoy the companionship of those who call on the Lord with pure hearts" (2 Tim. 2:22, NLT).

Living It Out

Pray these words from Psalm 51:10: "Create in me a pure heart, O God, and renew a steadfast spirit within me." As you strive for purity of body and heart, seek to follow the example of Jesus by approaching your life of purity with an attitude of humility.

DAY THIRTY-SEVEN

Pure as Snow

"Come now, let us reason together," says the LORD. "Though your sins are like scarlet, they shall be as white as snow; though they are red as crimson, they shall be like wool."

—Isaiah 1:18

Reflection

I absolutely love the Christmas season. There's something special about it—it's a very powerful, very moving time for me. I love gathering with family to celebrate the birth of our King, Jesus. I love decorating the tree while listening to Christmas music. Growing up, I loved to listen to Amy Grant's *Home for Christmas* album while we trimmed the tree.

My most memorable Christmas dinner was at Shannon Park just outside, Toowoomba, Queensland, Australia. On several occasions my family had Christmastime reunions at that campsite. We had lamb, turkey, and ham at the table, with relatives all around. I have about twenty-four cousins, and a good many of them were there. We wore brightly colored Christmas hats and pulled apart bonbons to find little treasures waiting inside. We talked and laughed and just had a wonderful time of fellowship together. My grandfather, who is a minister, always prayed, and then we talked about the true meaning of Christmas. It was a truly beautiful time.

On very rare occasions, snow is reported in Queensland.

Now that I live in Nashville, Tennessee, I see snow more frequently. At times I tour in the northeast part of America, and I get to see beautiful blankets of snow covering whole fields. What a beautiful sight that is!

You may have set out to remain sexually pure before marriage but somewhere along the way something happened. You fell short of God's standard and went further than you ever thought you would. You felt guilty and ashamed and have asked for God's forgiveness more than once. What now? Do you realize that you can still be considered clean in His sight? You may not be able to change the consequences that are a result of some bad choices, but if you've come to God and sought His forgiveness and mercy, you can be made as clean as a blanket of freshly fallen snow. He can make you pure again in His sight.

Looking Further

King David certainly knew what it was like to fall short in the area of sexual purity. He sinned by committing adultery with another man's wife, Bathsheba, then placed her husband, Uriah, on the front lines of battle so that he would be killed. This way (or so, David thought), his sin would be covered up. He found out that God is not to be mocked. God sent the prophet Nathan to confront him with the consequences of his actions. There is no sin that can be hidden from God. David suffered the consequences of his sin, and he confessed his wrongdoing to God in a very powerful psalm. In the midst of his declaration of guilt, he wrote these words:

> Purify me from my sins, and I will be clean; wash me, and
> I will be whiter than snow. (Ps. 51:7, NLT)

Living It Out

God is more than capable of turning the darkness of your sin into a blanket of pure snow. He simply asks that you come to Him in faith and true repentance, believing that what He says He will do He *will* accomplish. Don't allow the enemy to throw your past in your face; rather, bask in God's unquenchable grace and mercy.

DAY THIRTY-EIGHT

Setting Boundaries

God wants you to live a pure life. Keep yourselves from sexual promiscuity. Learn to appreciate and give dignity to your body, not abusing it, as is so common among those who know nothing of God. Don't run roughshod over the concerns of your brothers and sisters. Their concerns are God's concerns, and he will take care of them. We've warned you about this before. God hasn't invited us into a disorderly, unkempt life but into something holy and beautiful—as beautiful on the inside as the outside. If you disregard this advice, you're not offending your neighbors; you're rejecting God, who is making you a gift of his Holy Spirit.

—1 Thessalonians 4:3-8, THE MESSAGE

Reflection

So much of the secular world uses sex to sell music. Many young female musicians have people telling them, "Hey, you have to be more sexy, show more skin." And no matter how strong they often are at the start, eventually they allow themselves to be worn down. It's sad because they could be using their artistry and their talent—rather than their bodies—to sell their music. This approach is very damaging to the young guys and girls who are soaking it all in. Dressing immodestly and listening to music that encourages girls to be sexually active outside marriage can lead to all kinds of troubles, including physical and emotional consequences. My advice to you: Run!

I feel that we women have a responsibility not to tempt our brothers in Christ. We really need to help them out in the lust department. We need to be careful and wise in the clothes choices we make. I have set certain boundaries for myself in the way I dress. It can be a real challenge at times to find things that are modern and funky and "today" but still have an element of modesty. I try to take advantage of the unique locations I get to visit. Europe has great clothes—and I love to shop there.

"How far is too far?" If our goal is to honor God with our bodies, then we will draw the line and ask God for the strength not to cross it. One basic principle I live by and often share with others is to not let a guy touch me in any area that a swim-suit would cover. That goes for touching guys as well. A good question to ask is always, "If I participate in this activity, will I have a hard time explaining to my future spouse what I did with someone else?"

Once you've set physical boundaries, communicate them to the guy you are dating. Talk about what your boundaries are going to be as a couple. Pray together and ask God to help you honor Him in your relationship. Focus on the friendship, and don't rush anything. If the guy is worth waiting for, he'll wait for you. If you live by these guidelines, they will help keep you pure, and, more important, you'll be honoring God with your body.

Looking Further

Here are a few more Scriptures to aid you in setting physical boundaries:

- "Among you there must not be even a hint of sexual immorality, or of any kind of impurity, or of greed, because these are improper for God's holy people" (Eph. 5:3).
- "Stay away from every kind of evil" (1 Thess. 5:22, NLT).
- "The Lord is faithful; he will strengthen you and guard you from the evil one" (2 Thess. 3:3, NLT).
- "Honor marriage, and guard the sacredness of sexual intimacy between wife and husband. God draws a firm line against casual and illicit sex" (Heb. 13:4, THE MESSAGE).

Living It Out

If you're dating someone, have you determined physical boundaries, and have you communicated them to each other? If not, that conversation is a good place to start. Then ask God for the strength to stand strong. To not set boundaries ahead of time is to actually act as if there are *no* boundaries, which is just asking for trouble.

DAY THIRTY-NINE

Learning from Others' Examples

You don't want to end your life full of regrets, nothing but sin and bones, say-ing, "Oh, why didn't I do what they told me? Why did I reject a disciplined life? Why didn't I listen to my mentors, or take my teachers seriously?"
—Proverbs 5:11-13, THE MESSAGE

Reflection

As you travel along the journey in your quest to live a pure and devoted life, it may be helpful to follow the examples of others who have gone before you. I look up to heroes who have shown me how to navigate this journey of life. A mentor is someone who can guide and coach you, a tutor who has blazed the trail before you. One of my mentors is Evie Tornquist-Karlsson. She began in the Christian music industry while still a teen-ager, as I did, and she experienced many of the same pressures along the way. My family has known her for years and highly respects her Christian walk. Evie was a natural mentor for me. She even held me as a baby while she toured through Australia. She is an amazing woman of God. We get along well as kin-dred spirits with similar personalities, similar giftings, a love for people, a love for God, and a desire to please Him. Because she lives in Florida and I live in Tennessee, we most often com-municate through phone and e-mail, each of us asking how we can be praying for the other. Her voice of understanding is so valuable in my life.

Recently, a friend and life coach named Ken has influenced my life greatly. He's encouraged me to read books that have powerfully impacted me spiritually, including *Inner Voice of Love*, by Henri Nouwen; and François Fénelon's *Let Go*. Ken encourages me to see God's grace and love for me, and not merely God's justice and holiness. I grew up in a world saturated with Christianity, which is not a bad thing, but for a long time I think I bought into the "dos and don'ts" system—a legalistic form of Christianity. Through this coaching relationship with Ken, I've come to focus more on God as my Father. He really is loving, and He wants the best for me. This revelation has been very renewing in my walk with God.

When I think about Bible heroes, my mind turns to Ruth. She was someone for whom life held serious challenges. Her life didn't quite turn out as she hoped it would. During a famine in the land of Moab, she married, and then her husband died. But she kept her heart focused on trusting her God and was loyal to Him and to her mother-in-law, Naomi (who was also a widow)—even when given the option of returning to her home after her husband's death. Naomi mentored her daughter-in-law Ruth in the ways of her God. Eventually God rewarded Ruth's faithfulness by bringing another husband to her, and through him she had a son who became part of the bloodline of Jesus. I desire to imitate the loyalty and faithfulness of Ruth.

Every woman needs another woman who really understands what she feels and the pressures she faces. Every woman needs someone else with whom she can openly and honestly share life. And when a mentor has walked that same road before her, there is the assurance that there will be acceptance, compassion, and powerful prayers offered on her behalf.

Looking Further

The apostle Paul called Timothy his "son in the faith" (1 Tim. 1:2) because he mentored him in spreading the good news of Jesus as described throughout the pages of the New Testament. Paul was the teacher, Timothy the learner. Everybody needs a Paul, and everybody needs a Timothy. At any point in our lives we should be mentoring others, and there should also be people to whom we're looking for guidance, because we'll never be at a place where we have nothing else to learn.

Living It Out

Do you have a spiritual mentor in your life right now? What specific issues do you need to bring to her attention for prayer? If you do not presently have a mentor who regularly speaks into your life, begin praying that God will bring such a person to you. Then look for His answer.

DAY FORTY

While You Wait

The LORD must wait for you to come to him so he can show you his love and compassion. For the LORD is a faithful God. Blessed are those who wait for his help.

—Isaiah 30:18, NLT

Reflection

Besides simply being obedient to God's will for my life, another reason I want to keep my body pure is for my future husband, as a gift to him on our wedding night. For a while now I've been in the waiting stage, wanting to meet that one man God has for me. It's definitely a desire of my heart to get married and have a family, but I don't think God has brought that man into my life yet! I'm excited to see what God will do in that area of my life—hopefully in the not-too-distant future.

As you work through this waiting stage with me, I want to encourage you to not dwell on wishing your future husband were in your life right now. Instead, thank God for the good things in your life. A thankful heart leads to a positive, hope-filled life. If you or I were to just go out and try to make something happen with the wrong guy, it would do way more harm than good. I've known people who married the wrong person out of fear of loneliness, or purely for sexual reasons. And the results can be disastrous!

We don't need to run ahead of God. He knows our needs and has our best interests at heart. If God so chooses, I want

Him to bring the right man into my life. I know it's going to be a miracle for me to meet somebody who has a similar life experience and can relate to the circumstances I face every day. I believe he is going to have to be a really unique man. But I'm waiting for God to do this miracle for me, and I don't want to get in the way. I'm committed to trusting Him, no matter what does or doesn't come my way.

Looking Further

✓ In Psalm 37:4, David said, "Take delight in the LORD, and he will give you your heart's desires" (NLT).

✓ In Matthew 6:8, Jesus promised, "Your Father knows exactly what you need even before you ask him!" (NLT).

If you delight yourself in God first and foremost, He will take care of the future. No one ever said it would be easy to wait for God's plans for our future, but if we place our total trust in Him, it is possible to not just endure the wait but actually enjoy it!

Living It Out

While we wait, what should we do? Sit around as hopeless females twiddling our thumbs? Absolutely not. We can do many productive things during this waiting period. We can work on growing great relationships in our family and with close friends. We can learn to practice unselfishness by helping to meet others' needs. We can work on developing positive character traits that will help us now and benefit our future spouses later. We can enjoy pursuing hobbies. I love chilling out at a café with a friend, swimming, swing dancing, and bargain hunting. And we can pray for our future spouses, that God will keep their hearts and bodies pure for us. Get busy enjoying life.

DAY FORTY-ONE

Your Body Image

Fear not, for I have redeemed you; I have summoned you by name; you are mine. My verse

—Isaiah 43:1

Reflection

I've done my share of photo shoots for magazines and have had the benefit of hair and makeup stylists. You'd think I would be able to look at some of those images and say to myself, *Well, I look okay in that. I feel good about myself.* But I struggle like almost every other woman I know. I sometimes measure myself against models and actresses, even though so many of these women are unhealthily thin. Delighting in who God made us to be is hard. It's a daily battle, but one we can win that will aid us in feeling good about ourselves—and that confidence often makes it easier to stand for purity.

A few years ago, I broke up with my boyfriend. It was a difficult time, so I didn't eat much. Consequently I became really skinny. Even then I wanted to lose more weight. It's awful to be constantly unhappy with how you look. Yet how many women are guilty of that? I think we've got to make the best with what we have. Yes, we need to care for our bodies by exercising regularly and eating healthfully, but we can't let body-image issues rule our lives. I've been guilty of letting this preoccupy my thoughts. It's something I'm seeking God about.

The key to winning this battle is in reminding ourselves that God cherishes us just as we are. We must try to build our self-image around what God thinks of us. This requires spending time with Him regularly to allow Him to fill us with His love. It's also very important to have friends and family around who allow us to be honest with them and say, "I'm really struggling in this area. Pray for me today because I'm obsessing about this."

I love the way actress Reese Witherspoon put this struggle into perspective. She said, "You know what? I'm never going to win the skinny race. I'm never going to win the successful race. I just want to be the best me I can be." I love that. That's my goal. God really does delight in us as His daughters. We are valuable because we belong to the King.

Looking Further

In the Old Testament, we learn that God took His holy places very seriously. The Israelites had to follow strict regulations in regard to setting up the tabernacle in the wilderness. And the instructions God gave Solomon for building the temple in Jerusalem were very exact and had to be followed to the letter. Now, God delights in us so much that He chooses to view each of our bodies as a temple, a place fit for Him to dwell. That's something we may take for granted, but it's a pretty incredible thought.

First Corinthians 6:19-20 asks, "Didn't you realize that your body is a sacred place, the place of the Holy Spirit? Don't you see that you can't live however you please, squandering what God paid such a high price for? The physical part of you is not some piece of property belonging to the spiritual part of you. God owns the whole works. So let people see God in and through your body" (THE MESSAGE).

Living It Out

Where do you struggle the most with your body image? Not eating right? Not exercising regularly? Abusing your body with some habitual sin? Constantly comparing your physical appearance to others'? Whatever the case, realize that God has redeemed you. Write these phrases in crayon on your bathroom mirror: "God delights in me. God cherishes me. I am precious to Him." Let those truths sink into your mind for a solid week and see how they change your perspective.

DAY FORTY-TWO

Life Together

Let us think of ways to motivate one another to acts of love and good works. And let us not neglect our meeting together, as some people do, but encourage one another, especially now that the day of his return is drawing near.

—Hebrews 10:24-25, NLT

Reflection

Because of the international focus of my ministry, I've traveled to bring encouragement to Christians in some pretty dark places. I've seen some gorgeous cathedrals and church buildings; in many there is no longer an active body of Christ. The church is not about magnificent architecture, but rather an active, breathing body that sustains each of its members. Brothers and sisters lifting one another up in the journey of faith.

If there is an area of sexual purity you're struggling with, confide in someone you trust so you can receive the encouragement and accountability that come from a godly friendship. Make sure you choose someone who will accept you as you are and not judge you. At the same time, your confidant needs to be someone who has earned the right to speak truth into your life, someone who has a relationship with God and knows you very well.

God designed us to live in community with one another. He knows that we need each other in order to make it. One of the favorite ploys of the enemy is to attack us while we're vulnerable, while we're alone. He knows that none of us are a match for him without the support of God's strength and good Christian friends who encourage us to walk wisely. Get involved in a community of faith, the local body of Christ, where you can be encouraged to pray and to seek God with all your heart. These days on earth are short; they're numbered. Let's seize the day and be radical for God. We will make it by encouraging one another every step of the way.

Looking Further

Living in community the way God intends can be effectively carried out by "one anothering" each other. The apostle Paul challenged the churches of the New Testament to live out these truths, which are still appropriate for us today:

✔ "Be devoted to one another in brotherly love. Honor one another above yourselves" (Rom. 12:10).

✔ "Live in harmony with each other. Don't be too proud to enjoy the company of ordinary people. And don't think you know it all!" (Rom. 12:16, NLT).

✔ "Accept one another, then, just as Christ accepted you, in order to bring praise to God" (Rom. 15:7).

✔ "I myself am convinced, my brothers, that you yourselves are full of goodness, complete in knowledge and competent to instruct one another" (Rom. 15:14).

✔ "Make me truly happy by agreeing wholeheartedly with each other, loving one another, and working together with one mind and purpose" (Phil. 2:2, NLT).

✔ "Let the Word of Christ—the Message—have the run of the house. Give it plenty of room in your lives. Instruct and direct one another using good common sense" (Col. 3:16, THE MESSAGE).

✔ "Speak encouraging words to one another. Build up hope so you'll all be together in this, no one left out, no one left behind. I know you're already doing this; just keep on doing it" (1 Thess. 5:11, THE MESSAGE).

Living It Out

If you have someone in your life with whom you can be vulnerable, what do you need to say today? Is God calling you to encourage someone in her walk toward purity? Be available to listen, and speak God's truths as you are prompted.

DAY FORTY-THREE

The Power of His Forgiveness

If you, GOD, kept records on wrongdoings, who would stand a chance? As it turns out, forgiveness is your habit, and that's why you're worshiped.

—Psalm 130:3-4, THE MESSAGE

Reflection

Quite a few years ago I recorded a song called "Go and Sin No More," which was based on Jesus' encounter with the woman caught in adultery (see John 8:3-11). She had been captured by the angry mob and thrown at Jesus' feet. The accusers had already convicted her of sin in their hearts, and they wanted to stone her as a judgment for that sin. But Jesus had a different perspective, one of forgiveness. He challenged the mob to let the man without sin step forward from their midst and cast the first stone. Stunned by His declaration, one by one those in the crowd dropped their stones and walked away. Lifting the woman to her feet, Jesus looked into her eyes and said, "Woman, where are your accusers?" Looking around in amazement, she saw that none of her accusers remained to stone her for her sin. "Neither do I condemn you," said Jesus. "Go and sin no more."

This is a beautiful example of the power of God's forgiveness! It's a message that applies to each of us, no matter what we've done. "Forgive me" are two words vital to our daily relationship with God. When we give our lives to Jesus, His Spirit comes to live within us and begins to change and renew us from the inside out. It takes discipline to yield our human wills to God's will for us, because our human nature keeps creeping in, doesn't it? Even the apostle Paul experienced this ongoing battle. "For what I do is not the good I want to do," he wrote in Romans 7:19. "No, the evil I do not want to do—this I keep on doing."

This is where God's forgiveness really becomes amazing grace toward us. We were forgiven through the shed blood of God's own Son when we accepted the gift of salvation and eternal life that came to us through Jesus' death on the cross. God is faithful to forgive us anew each time we come to Him, truly repent, and ask for His forgiveness. Forgiveness is a free gift from God, but the cost to Him was tremendous. He has paid for our forgiveness through the sacrifice of His own dear Son.

Looking Further

Even after we realize we have received God's forgiveness, sometimes it is a very hard thing to forgive ourselves. My song "Forgive Me" says this: "For all the times I've failed You, Lord . . . for all the times I've fallen short . . . forgive me."[10] These are words we need to remember. A pure heart before God is the lifeline to our spiritual walk with Him. And by speaking two small words, "Forgive me," we avail ourselves of God's unending supply of forgiveness and mercy.

Living It Out

None of us are perfect this side of heaven. When you stumble in your daily walk (whether in thoughts, words, or deeds), immediately acknowledge your need for forgiveness, seek God's forgiveness with a repentant heart, and ask Him to draw you even closer to Him as you continue on your journey. Are there sins in your life for which you have never felt truly forgiven? List them—and ask God today to forgive you! He promises that He will (see 1 John 1:9).

DAY FORTY-FOUR

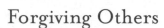

Forgiving Others

In prayer there is a connection between what God does and what you do. You can't get forgiveness from God, for instance, without also forgiving others. If you refuse to do your part, you cut yourself off from God's part.

—Matthew 6:14-15, THE MESSAGE

Reflection

As a wise Father, God teaches us not only how crucial it is to be truly forgiven but also the importance of forgiving others. Jesus knew this was of such significance to our relationship with the Father that He voiced this as an example to His followers in the Lord's Prayer. If you obey His directive to forgive others who have offended you, you will truly be following Jesus' example of showing godly love for one another.

Matthew 5:23-24; 18:15-17 spells out the correct way to go about reconciling with someone who has offended you. If you've offended someone, perhaps in the area of sexual purity, or any offense for that matter, go to that person (or write a letter, if going in person is not advisable), and ask for that person's forgiveness with a sincere heart. In twelve-step groups, this is often known as making amends. It's much more than simply saying, "I'm sorry." It indicates a real heart's desire to make a serious change, and a commitment to follow through on the promise.

[handwritten margin note: But isn't this what (I'm sorry) means?]

Someone may have taken advantage of you in the past in some way. You can't change what they did to you, but you can determine what you will do about it. And, forgiveness is the best option. Unforgiveness is a prison, but you hold the keys. Unlock your heart by asking God to help you forgive and to give you love in place of unforgiveness. Then you will be free to enjoy a close walk with God.

Looking Further

Forgiving others is perhaps one of the most difficult tasks many Christians struggle with. Maybe that's why the New Testament has so much to say on the subject. Here's a sampling:

- "The master called the servant in. 'You wicked servant,' he said, 'I canceled all that debt of yours because you begged me to. Shouldn't you have had mercy on your fellow servant just as I had on you?' In anger his master turned him over to the jailers to be tortured, until he should pay back all he owed. 'This is how my heavenly Father will treat each of you unless you forgive your brother from your heart'" (Matt. 18:32-35).
- "When you are praying, first forgive anyone you are holding a grudge against, so that your Father in heaven will forgive your sins, too" (Mark 11:25, NLT).

"Be alert. If you see your friend going wrong, correct him. If he responds, forgive him. Even if it's personal against you and repeated seven times through the day, and seven times he says, 'I'm sorry, I won't do it again,' forgive him" (Luke 17:3-4, THE MESSAGE).

"Be gentle with one another, sensitive. Forgive one another as quickly and thoroughly as God in Christ forgave you" (Eph. 4:32, THE MESSAGE).

"Make allowance for each other's faults, and forgive anyone who offends you. Remember, the Lord forgave you, so you must forgive others" (Col. 3:13, NLT).

In the Lord's mind, it's a nonnegotiable. Simply put, we are to forgive others. Period.

Living It Out

Are there people in your life whom you have offended—and whom you need to ask for their forgiveness? Ask God to bring them to your remembrance and to give you the courage to reach out and ask for pardon.

Do you need to forgive someone else? No matter how deep the wound, God calls you to offer forgiveness. In order to follow Jesus' example, you must forgive. With God's help you can do anything—even this.

DAY FORTY-FIVE

Modest Is Hottest

I want women to be modest in their appearance. They should wear decent and appropriate clothing and not draw attention to themselves by the way they fix their hair or by wearing gold or pearls or expensive clothes. For women who claim to be devoted to God should make themselves attractive by the good things they do.

—1 Timothy 2:9-10, NLT

Reflection

One of my most embarrassing moments ever came while I was touring Europe. I was doing a concert in Wales. On one particular night the people at the show seemed very distant. I should have thought at the time, *There's probably a good reason they're acting that way.* I was wearing a black skirt over some pants that night. The skirt had red stitching with an "s" pattern all over it. At the end of the show, a girl came through the autograph line and asked, "Did you know that your skirt spells 'sex' over and over again?" I was mortified because I didn't know that's what the pattern said. As usual I had talked about my virginity and the call for sexual abstinence during the concert. I asked the girl, "Do you know if very many people noticed this?" And she said, "Well, it kind of was going around at intermission." I was humiliated and wanted to sink into the floor.

Inadvertently, that skirt broadcast a message completely opposed to what I had been singing about, and not at all what I had hoped to communicate. That brings up a really good question: Are the words you say consistent with what you are wearing and how you act?

I saw a T-shirt that read "Modest is hottest." That's a great motto. Modesty means way more than just *not* dressing provocatively. The word *modesty* has to do with walking in humility, being meek and unassuming. Someone who is modest places a moderate estimate on her abilities, is not bold or in-your-face, is not vain or conceited.

In contrast to those who seem to be full of themselves, modesty really is hottest—it's attractive to others because people know that a modest person is more concerned about others than about herself. A modest person usually prefers that others be in the spotlight. She'd rather take a behind-the-scenes role. In my profession this can be a struggle as performers are constantly thrust into the spotlight. Because of that, modesty is an attitude I am always working on. But just because we seek to be modest does not mean we are weak. In fact, a modest person may be very self-confident because she is comfortable with who she is and doesn't have to spend all her time proving herself to others.

Looking Further

Our model is Jesus, who was strong but meek, confident but compassionate, and knowledgeable in every way yet humble. Paul challenges us to have the same modest attitude as Jesus:

> Don't push your way to the front; don't sweet-talk your way to the top. Put yourself aside, and help others get ahead. Don't be obsessed with getting your own advantage. Forget yourselves long enough to lend a helping hand.

Think of yourselves the way Christ Jesus thought of himself. He had equal status with God but didn't think so much of himself that he had to cling to the advantages of that status no matter what. Not at all. When the time came, he set aside the privileges of deity and took on the status of a slave, became *human*! Having become human, he stayed human. It was an incredibly humbling process. He didn't claim special privileges. Instead, he lived a selfless, obedient life and then died a selfless, obedient death—and the worst kind of death at that: a crucifixion. (Phil. 2:3-8, THE MESSAGE)

And James wrote about this too:

Do you want to be counted wise, to build a reputation for wisdom? Here's what you do: Live well, live wisely, live humbly. It's the way you live, not the way you talk, that counts. . . . Real wisdom, God's wisdom, begins with a holy life and is characterized by getting along with others. It is gentle and reasonable, overflowing with mercy and blessings, not hot one day and cold the next, not two-faced. (James 3:13, 17, THE MESSAGE)

Living It Out

Spend some time thinking about how you live, how you dress, and the way you talk. Is the message you convey through each of these aspects of your life consistent, or are you ever two-faced? Would people who know you best use words like *modest* and *humble* to describe you? If not, what can you do to change their perception?

DAY FORTY-SIX

Preventing the Fall

These are all warning markers—DANGER!—in our history books, written down so that we don't repeat their mistakes. Our positions in the story are parallel—they at the beginning, we at the end—and we are just as capable of messing it up as they were. Don't be so naive and self-confident. You're not exempt. You could fall flat on your face as easily as anyone else. Forget about self-confidence; it's useless. Cultivate God-confidence.

—1 Corinthians 10:11-12, THE MESSAGE

Reflection

There is such an attack today on purity. It's everywhere. It's rampant. Every Christian leader must be vigilant, committed to God and committed to purity. From time to time we read of a high-profile Christian leader who has had a "moral failure." People are often shocked when this occurs, wondering how that person's life ever spiraled so far downward. The answer usually is, "Little by little." Christians are quick to elevate people to pedestals, but they don't really know their hearts and their private lives—only God does. And the truth is that none of us in our own flesh are any better than anyone else. We're all in desperate need of God's grace.

What's the cure for stopping these moral tragedies from happening? As long as people are human, there are no guarantees, but asking ourselves questions that will help us guard our hearts is certainly a good place to start. We must ask ourselves if watching something on TV, at the movies, or on the Internet is helpful to our spiritual walk. What we put in our hearts and our minds is going to come out in our actions. We must also be careful not to put ourselves in compromising situations. We are told in the Bible to avoid "every kind of evil" (1 Thess. 5:22, NLT).

Then we must be very intentional about accountability. The enemy is prowling around like a roaring lion, and he wants to destroy us (see 1 Pet. 5:8). One of his favorite targets is in the area of sexual purity. The way to defeat him is by learning specific Scriptures that can help us in our defense, and by choosing to make ourselves accountable to others who have our best interests at heart. We need to let others know what's going on in our lives. For example, if you must travel alone on business, make sure your accountability partners know with whom you will be traveling and where you will be. The enemy knows that we are more vulnerable when we are removed from our support systems. All too often that is when believers get themselves into trouble. Vulnerability to others leads to strength. It's the most free and joyful way, and the way that pleases God.

Looking Further

In times of temptation, meditate on these verses, and ask for God's strength to be victorious:

- "He will cover you with his feathers. He will shelter you with his wings. His faithful promises are your armor and protection" (Ps. 91:4, NLT).
- "Don't let us yield to temptation, but rescue us from the evil one" (Matt. 6:13, NLT).
- "No test or temptation that comes your way is beyond the

course of what others have had to face. All you need to re-member is that God will never let you down; he'll never let you be pushed past your limit; he'll always be there to help you come through it" (1 Cor. 10:13, THE MESSAGE).

Living It Out

What safeguards do you have in place to prevent yourself from falling morally? Are there specific people in your life to whom you have made your actions accountable? Do you know your areas of potential weakness? Are there specific places you need to avoid? Talk to God today about your desire to be pure in mind, body, and spirit. Ask Him for strength during times of temptation, and believe that He will come to your aid. You can believe it because it's true!

DAY FORTY-SEVEN

The Benefits of Abstinence

Dear friends, I urge you, as aliens and strangers in the world, to abstain from sinful desires, which war against your soul. Live such good lives among the pagans that, though they accuse you of doing wrong, they may see your good deeds and glorify God on the day he visits us.

—I Peter 2:11-12

Reflection

We live in a totally "if it feels good, do it" world. We constantly hear messages from others such as "Condoms work as an alternative" and "Oral sex is not really sex." Both of these statements are false. Even in the face of the risk of HIV and the more than 15 million new STD infections diagnosed each year, 33 percent of eight- to eleven-year-olds and 49 percent of twelve- to fifteen-year-olds say that the pressure to have sex is a big problem for them.[11] Unfortunately, our society tells us we have to have sex to be happy and fulfilled.

Sexual relationships outside marriage are the accepted norm on the vast majority of TV shows and movies that we watch. And, marketing executives know all too well that "sex sells" their products in TV and magazine advertisements. Teen pregnancies and abortions have scarred untold numbers of lives with consequences that last a lifetime. Too many have found out the hard way that sex, when indulged in outside marriage, only satisfies for a short time, while its consequences live on.

Abstinence from sex before marriage is the only guaranteed protection.

I'm passionate about this issue because I've seen so many of my generation and the one coming up behind us ripped off. We've been sold the lie that it doesn't matter how we choose to handle sex—but there is a huge cost for living so liberally. We need to warn others of the consequences by saying, "Don't go along with the lie. Here's why God's way is the better way." The benefits of abstinence far outweigh the short-lived pleasure of sexual activity outside marriage:

- You won't have to explain your past to your spouse.
- You don't have to be concerned about acquiring HIV or an STD.
- You won't have to deal with regret, guilt, fear of commitment, and other emotional consequences.
- You don't have to worry about how it will affect your Christian witness.
- You'll know that you are in the center of God's will in this area of your life.

The facts are clear. It seems pretty obvious. Why would we want to pursue any direction other than God's way?

Looking Further

It seems as though the apostle Paul confronted the enemy's sexual perversions wherever he traveled. He had some hard-hitting words for the followers of Christ who were striving to remain pure in the midst of a depraved society. After speaking about sexual purity in his first letter to them, he wrote again to the

Corinthians in his second letter: "Yes, I am afraid that when I come again, God will humble me in your presence. And I will be grieved because many of you have not given up your old sins. You have not repented of your impurity, sexual immorality, and eagerness for lustful pleasure" (2 Cor. 12:21, NLT).

And to the Galatian believers, Paul urged:

> Let the Holy Spirit guide your lives. Then you won't be doing what your sinful nature craves. The sinful nature wants to do evil, which is just the opposite of what the Spirit wants. And the Spirit gives us desires that are the opposite of what the sinful nature desires. These two forces are constantly fighting each other, so you are not free to carry out your good intentions. But when you are directed by the Spirit, you are not under obligation to the law of Moses. When you follow the desires of your sinful nature, the results are very clear: sexual immorality, impurity, lustful pleasures . . . (Gal. 5:16-19, NLT)

Living It Out

Have you received any messages from the media about sex that you need to *unlearn*? As you read the above list of benefits concerning sexual abstinence before marriage, which one spoke most clearly to you? Is there someone in your life who needs to hear that God's way is the best way? Pray, and look for an opportunity to have a conversation with that person today.

DAY FORTY-EIGHT

Loving Transformation

Mostly what God does is love you. Keep company with him and learn a life of love. Observe how Christ loved us. His love was not cautious but extravagant. He didn't love in order to get something from us but to give everything of him-self to us. Love like that.

—Ephesians 5:2, THE MESSAGE

Reflection

It's been my goal for some time to play an acting part in a musi-cal, and a few years ago I got the opportunity. I played the role of Maggie in the rock opera *!Hero*, which was a very state-of-the-art production. This character was sort of a mix between two people in the Bible, Mary Magdalene and the woman at the well. I think God provided me with a unique way to understand the part of this girl from the streets. Because of my message of sexual abstinence through the years, I have come in contact with a lot of "Maggies" who came from varied pasts. They've shared with me in depth about the emotional consequences of having sex outside marriage and how their lives have been scarred in so many painful ways—similar to the life of the character in the musical.

When my character first came out onstage it was obvious she was cold and hard and angry. People were in shock when I ap-peared in a fairly provocative outfit. !Hero (Jesus, played by Michael Tait) knew the secrets of her heart, and initially she was very resistant to that. Maggie was a girl desperately wanting to reach out and believe the truth Jesus offered her. She saw that He was offering her true life and real love, so she became one of His followers.

When I studied Mary Magdalene, I was impressed with how loving and respectful she was toward Jesus. I sensed the reverence she had for Him. I really enjoyed playing Maggie's role because she gives hope to all of us. Jesus first encountered her when she was a sinful woman of the streets, and He made a radical transformation in her life. She realized how much she needed the life He had to offer. As the story unfolded, she became a soft and loving woman who was very protective of Jesus. I love the grace and love Jesus showed to her. He offers that same grace and love to you and me!

Looking Further

Mary was from the city of Magdala, an important trading center on the northwest shore of the Sea of Galilee. Luke tells us that Jesus cast seven demons out of her (see Luke 8:2). She could never forget how He lovingly rescued her, so she became one of Jesus' most devoted followers and was part of a group of women who served Him out of their resources. She accompanied Him and His disciples when He went to Jerusalem just prior to His death, was present at the foot of the cross, came to the tomb to anoint Jesus' body, reported the fact that the tomb was empty, and gave the angels' message to the disciples.

Mary Magdalene had the distinction of being the first person Jesus appeared to after His resurrection. She had come back to the gravesite after taking her message of the empty tomb to Peter and John. She returned with them; then, after the disciples went back home, she stood by the tomb weeping (see John 20:10-11). She began talking with someone she supposed was the gardener. When Jesus called her by her name, she immediately recognized Him as her risen Lord. No doubt she spent the rest of her earthly days telling people her story of loving transformation.

Living It Out

Have you heard the Lord whisper your name lately? What has He spoken to you? Spend some moments today praising Him for what He's accomplished in your life and asking Him to continue to transform you into the image of His Son.

DAY FORTY-NINE

Above Reproach

LORD, we show our trust in you by obeying your laws; our heart's desire is to glorify your name.

—Isaiah 26:8, NLT

Reflection

There are a couple of practical things that can really help us in our pursuit of purity. If we truly want to please God with our lives, we will realize that God is watching us all the time. A good question to ask is always, "How would God feel about what I am doing right now?" A second helpful question is, "Am I glorifying God in all my actions?" As you ask yourself these questions, pray to God for the strength to stand strong. As devoted followers of Jesus, we are called to a higher standard. We must live above reproach.

I was so impressed with Billy Graham's policy of never riding in a car with someone of the opposite sex (besides his wife) unless someone else was present that I have adopted that policy myself. Once while I was on tour, a driver came to transport me from my hotel to the concert hall, and I sent him back to get a third person to ride with us. Not too long ago I went to a single guy's house to work on a song with him. But I didn't go alone. It's not that I didn't trust this guy. He and I both understood that we needed someone else to be there. I know to some people these guidelines might seem rather silly, but I don't want anyone to be able to accuse me of not walking the talk.

I want to be consistent whether I'm on the stage or off. As the oldest of seven kids, I've always had a sense of responsibility. I desire to live a life that honors and glorifies God, and my role as an artist encourages me to live even more radically for Him. A Saint Francis of Assisi quote, "Preach the gospel at all times—if necessary, use words," has really been an inspiration to me. None of us are perfect, but it is so important that we strive to live what we say we believe.

Looking Further

The Greek word we translate "glorify," *doxazo*, originally meant "to render or esteem glorious; honor; magnify."[12] It is often used in the Psalms to refer to praising God with our voices in song. But in a larger sense, it means to glorify God with our whole lives. From the root of this word we derive the title of one of the most well-known hymns ever composed, "The Doxology," whose lyrics were written by Thomas Ken in 1674.[13] We glorify the Father, Son, and Holy Ghost when we choose to live above reproach.

One of the ways we help our brothers and sisters glorify God in their lives is by helping them treat their bodies with honor and respect. It's our responsibility to help one another live in ways that are pleasing to God. The apostle Paul offered these words:

✓ "May the God who gives endurance and encouragement give you a spirit of unity among yourselves as you follow Christ Jesus, so that with one heart and mouth you may glorify the God and Father of our Lord Jesus Christ" (Rom. 15:5-6).

✓ "We pray this so that the name of our Lord Jesus may be glorified in you, and you in him, according to the grace of our God and the Lord Jesus Christ" (2 Thess. 1:12).

Living It Out

Pray this simple prayer today: "God, I want to glorify You with my mind, heart, and body. Teach me what it means to magnify Your name through my thoughts and actions. Help me live above reproach."

DAY FIFTY

The Romance of Waiting

Christ has set us free to live a free life. So take your stand! Never again let anyone put a harness of slavery on you. . . . It is absolutely clear that God has called you to a free life. Just make sure that you don't use this freedom as an excuse to do whatever you want to do and destroy your freedom. Rather, use your freedom to serve one another in love; that's how freedom grows.

—Galatians 5:1, 13, THE MESSAGE

Reflection

Deep down, many young people know that waiting until marriage for sex is the right way to go, and they just want encouragement to wait. The majority of girls I have met are such romantics at heart and really want to be strong in this area. Many young women have chosen to write letters to their future spouses. Maybe you've done the same. If not, I'd encourage you to think about doing so. Creating something that you can one day give to your special someone will really help the waiting process. It's a pretty well-known fact that guys would like to marry a virgin. I think the whole idea that a girl is waiting appeals to them and helps them strive to be men of honor.

We are created by God to desire intimacy, to yearn for someone to know us completely and still love us. We want to share our hearts and lives with others. A guy is wired to protect; a girl longs to be protected. Romance has been very distorted by our culture today. The romance often portrayed in movies and on TV really is all about a short-lived sexual encounter. But the truth is that the most joyful, beautiful, exciting, and freeing romance is pure. It has nothing to do with selfish motives and desires or with short-term gratification. Rather, it is concerned with being free to love within the boundaries of God's perfect guidelines.

Standing strong with others is another key way in which you can win the battle for purity of body. Just about every time I hear of a young person who has slid down an immoral path, it's because he or she surrounded himself or herself with other young people who were not living the Christian life and were not committed to God's way. On the other hand, I've also seen a lot of young people who have waited, and I think a large reason why they've had the strength to stand strong is because they've dated other people who were also committed to waiting. I'd encourage you to choose this option. If you have friends who are also committed to waiting, you can encourage one another along the way!

Looking Further

The story of Isaac and Rebekah in the Bible is one of mystery and romance. After Isaac's mother, Sarah, died, Abraham sent his servant out to find a wife for his son Isaac from his homeland in Mesopotamia. As the servant stopped to rest at a well outside the town of Nahor, he encountered a woman who was "very beautiful, a virgin; no man had ever lain with her" (Gen. 24:16). After she gave him and his camels water to drink, the servant knew Rebekah was the one God had chosen, for he had prayed that God would validate His choice with a sign. The marriage was arranged, and Rebekah agreed to go back with the servant to marry Isaac, whom she had never met. She simply trusted the plan that God had put in place. "So she became [Isaac's] wife, and he loved her" (Gen. 24:67).

I'm not encouraging you to marry someone you've never met (such as an acquaintance from online dating or chat rooms). But, like Rebekah, you can trust in whatever God has planned for your future. And part of the fun is the mystery!

Living It Out

Is romance a concept you've given up on in today's world? Why or why not? God asks you to submit your dreams and desires of romance to His plan. He knows what is best, and His timing is always perfect. Trust Him.

DAY FIFTY-ONE

Mystery Man

He's already made it plain how to live, what to do, what GOD is looking for in men and women. It's quite simple: Do what is fair and just to your neighbor, be compassionate and loyal in your love, and don't take yourself too seriously—take God seriously.

—Micah 6:8, THE MESSAGE

Reflection

I've been asked many times what I look for in a guy I would like to marry. I don't have a long list, although I know some women who do. First and foremost, I want to be able to *see* his love for God. I want to know that God is the center of his life. This is really what makes a guy handsome in my eyes. I have this picture of him sitting at the table praying and reading his Bible. If he is the kind of guy who loves to be alone with God, that will challenge me to love God even more. Believing that he desires purity—which comes out of his close relationship with God—and is physically waiting for me, inspires me to continue to be sexually pure as well.

The guy for me is also going to have to love kids. I love seeing guys let little kids climb all over them. If he's good around small children, I think it says a lot about his character. It says he's the kind of guy who doesn't always think about pleasing himself. He cares about pleasing other people—especially little people! If God brings this man into my life, I envision the day when we'll have our own children and be able to pray with them at night and then tuck them into bed.

I don't know who this "mystery man" is, but I've written love letters to him. In these letters I address him as if I've known him for a long time. I write about things that are relevant to my life at that particular time, so that later he will be able to get a glimpse of what my life was like without him. It's fun to imagine what I think he might be like as a person, knowing that someday I'll find out how much I was on, or how far I was off!

Looking Further

In 1 Timothy 3, Paul gives Timothy a list of traits God looks for in godly men who want to be church leaders. Among the traits are the following: a life above reproach, self-control, a good reputation, respect, hospitality, no heavy drinking, gentleness, no quarreling, generosity, and integrity. In Titus 1, Paul enumerates a similar list that includes the following desirable qualities: blamelessness, no arrogance or quick temper, wisdom, honesty, holiness, and discipline.

Finding a man who possesses all these traits perfectly would be equivalent to finding Jesus, the perfect God-man. And even though humans will never achieve perfection in their lifetime, the aim should be to get as close as possible to exemplifying these qualities. For any man they are certainly goals worth shooting for. And for any woman, this is a man worth waiting for. God is looking for the man who can agree with the psalmist, "I will be careful to live a blameless life—when will you come to help me? I will lead a life of integrity in my own home" (Ps. 101:2, NLT).

Living It Out

Take a look at the qualities for godly men listed above. Which of these traits means the most to you in thinking about your relationships? Which of these traits is the most difficult for you to achieve? Why? Which would you most like to embody more in your life? Talk to God about your desires concerning this.

Day Fifty-two

Building Solid Marriages

*The L*ORD *God said, "It is not good for the man to be alone. I will make a helper who is just right for him." . . . "At last!" the man exclaimed. "This one is bone from my bone, and flesh from my flesh! She will be called 'woman,' because she was taken from 'man.' " This explains why a man leaves his father and mother and is joined to his wife, and the two are united into one.*

—Genesis 2:18, 23-24, NLT

Reflection

I was so fortunate to be raised by two godly parents who are still passionately in love with God and with each other. Their romance grew out of a four-year friendship. And in the past thirty-three years (and through seven kids) they have learned that their marriage was most successful when they learned to give, love, and serve each other more than they sought to receive. This is in direct contrast to the user mentality with which much of the world approaches relationships. Solid marriages are built on unconditional commitment and an attitude of selflessness, and I have seen that powerfully demonstrated in the lives of my parents.

My mum and dad were totally honest with each other and with us as we grew up. On the road in ministry we watched them live transparently with each other. We had amazing conversations about things like premarital sex, drugs, life mistakes, dating, and friends. I always knew that I could go to my mum with anything. I could totally trust her and know that she wasn't going to make light of anything I asked. My dad has always been there to give me godly counsel. He is so wise, and I have so much respect for all that he has been through and the life lessons he's learned. The united front they presented as parents was such an encouragement to my five brothers, my sister, and me as we grew up. My heart breaks for kids today who don't grow up with this kind of emotional support and spiritual foundation. The more we strive to build solid biblical marriages, the more victorious we will be in the battle for purity as kids watch us and are influenced by our example.

Looking Further

The apostle Paul gives advice to husbands and wives seeking to serve each other selflessly. He challenges us with these words:

> Out of respect for Christ, be courteously reverent to one another. Wives, understand and support your husbands in ways that show your support for Christ. The husband provides leadership to his wife the way Christ does to his church, not by domineering but by cherishing. So just as the church submits to Christ as he exercises such leadership, wives should likewise submit to their husbands. Husbands, go all out in your love for your wives, exactly as Christ did for the church—a love marked by giving, not getting. (Eph. 5:21-25, THE MESSAGE)

When a husband and a wife both seek to put the other's needs ahead of their own, powerful things happen. So many divorces today stem from individuals choosing not to place God's will and their spouse's needs above their own desires. Rather than letting Satan have a field day as he seeks to destroy yet another home, choose to live in a godly way by treating family members with kindness, humility, and grace. When you do, your home will be a place that shines the light of Jesus brightly.

Living It Out

What would God have you learn from the Ephesians passage about the way you should treat others with whom you have relationships? Talk to Him about your desire to be more concerned with giving to others than with getting.

DAY FIFTY-THREE

The Benefits of Singleness

An unmarried woman or virgin is concerned about the Lord's affairs: Her aim is to be devoted to the Lord in both body and spirit. But a married woman is concerned about the affairs of this world—how she can please her husband. I am saying this for your own good, not to restrict you, but that you may live in a right way in undivided devotion to the Lord.

—1 Corinthians 7:34-35

Reflection

From time to time I get discouraged as I wait for my future husband. In those times I try to focus on two things: First, a while back God gave me a vision of being happily married in the future, looking back on my single years, and thinking, *Why did I ever worry that God wouldn't look out for me? And what good did it do to worry?* Second, I try to focus on preparing to be a good wife. I want to build my intimacy with God so that He is the foundation of everything I am now and in the future.

God has called me to give my dream of being married completely over to Him. It was difficult, but I prayed, "God, I'll love You even if You don't provide this for me. And I'll trust that You know what's best for me." Even the thought of having to say that made me cry. But I really did come to realize God is God, and He knows me and loves me more intimately than anybody could. And if there's some reason in His divine purpose why I shouldn't be married, then He knows it. I trust He'll make happen in my life what's best for me. In this process, I've come to know such peace.

I'm not so naive as to think I won't ever struggle again or have days when I'm lonely. But on those lonely days, I know I'll have my strong community to lean on. And I'll fall back on what I know to be true, even when it might not *feel* true: God loves me, He knows what's best for me, and He has His reasons for what's happening in my life. And really, that's enough.

Looking Further

In I Corinthians 7, the apostle Paul lists the benefits of being single versus being married in this world:

- Your body belongs only to the Lord (v. 4).
- You have more time to devote to prayer and intimacy with God (v. 5).

✔ You can know the joy of fulfilling God's will for your life (v. 17).

✔ You will save yourself from troubles (v. 28).

✔ You can be singularly focused on how to please the Lord, rather than putting pleasing your spouse above pleasing God (vv. 32-34).

Getting married is not the solution to all of life's problems, as we singles can be tempted to think. Married people also struggle with loneliness and sexual temptation. And it is definitely worse to marry the wrong person than to not get married at all. Far too many people have settled for less than God would have for them by marrying rather than waiting for God's blessing, when perhaps in His timing He was trying to protect them from troubles in this world. God really does know us best and love us most. He is worth trusting in our present and future.

Living It Out

Whether you're single or married, it really boils down to the same thing. Have you surrendered your will and your future to God? It's a tough prayer to pray, but I encourage you to pray it every morning as you begin your day. You might pray something like this: "Lord, I lay this day and my future before You. I surrender my own desires to Your will for me." Why not start today?

DAY FIFTY-FOUR

A Lasting Legacy

Stand firm and hold to the teachings we passed on to you, whether by word of mouth or by letter.

—2 Thessalonians 2:15

Reflection

This past October, my maternal grandmother, Nanna, went home to be with Jesus. I cherished her dearly. Her name, Jean, was passed on to my mum as her middle name, and my parents passed it on to me as my middle name as well. Like Timothy, my faith first lived in my mum, and in my grandmother before that (see 2 Tim. 1:5). My grandmother was an incredible influence in my life, and in the lives of so many others. Nanna was a shining beacon for Jesus—His love and goodness. She and my maternal grandfather, Pops, were married for sixty years, which is quite an accomplishment! Her legacy of lovingly serving and nurturing people will live on for a long, long time.

On the topic of staying sexually pure before marriage, she had this to say: "Sex is sacred—don't let too much free action, free talk, or public displays of affection into your relationship. There is a fine line between purity and sexual liberty. Because our bodies are the temple of God, if we abuse the sacred gift of sex, then we are really abusing God's beautiful gift to us." She believed that one practical way to preserve sexual purity while dating was to not be isolated from others as a couple. She was a big advocate for going out with others in groups, which takes the pressure off and just allows people to be themselves in a casual environment. She felt that the most important thing in seeking a lifelong partner is to have a spiritual foundation in the relationship. And that was the secret to her many happy years with Pops.

Looking Further

Before the Bible was ever recorded in written format as we have it today, it was passed down through oral tradition, from generation to generation. When Moses gave God's moral code to the Israelites, he commanded them to pass on the laws and regulations of God's covenant to their children, who would pass them on to *their* children. When God brought His people into the Promised Land of Canaan, He commanded them to not intermarry with the pagan peoples surrounding them because He knew that ungodly influences would taint their beliefs in the one true God.

Asaph was one of King David's three Levitical choir leaders. These words about passing the baton of faith on to each generation are attributed to Asaph:

> O my people, listen to my instructions. Open your ears to what I am saying, for I will speak to you in a parable. I will teach you hidden lessons from our past—stories we have heard and known, stories our ancestors handed down to us. We will not hide these truths from our children; we will tell the next generation about the glorious deeds of the LORD, about his power and his mighty wonders . . . so the next generation might know them—even the children not yet born—and they in turn will teach their own children. So each generation should set its hope anew on

God, not forgetting his glorious miracles and obeying his commands. (Ps. 78:1-4, 6-7, NLT)

Living It Out

Who has left you a godly legacy to follow? What specific teachings did that person pass on that you are grateful for today? How have these words helped you walk in God's truth? To whom will you leave a lasting legacy, and what godly advice will you be remembered for?

DAY FIFTY-FIVE

Unselfish Love

Love never gives up. Love cares more for others than for self. Love doesn't want what it doesn't have. Love doesn't strut, doesn't have a swelled head, doesn't force itself on others, isn't always "me first."

—1 Corinthians 13:4-5, THE MESSAGE

Reflection

I was a young girl living in Australia when I first heard about her. I walked into the living room where my parents were watching a TV documentary about her life. From that time on, Mother Teresa has been one of my greatest heroes. Her love for God overflowed to others in extraordinary ways. It was so apparent in everything she did and said. She looked at every single person—the dying, the lepers, those rejected by society—as if they were Jesus. She wasn't afraid to touch them. They couldn't do anything to return her love, but she loved them anyway.

That's the kind of unconditional love we are called to have for others. Much of what is termed "love" in our culture is just the opposite. It is conditional, self-centered, and out only for what it can *get*. I've spoken with so many girls who were sorry after engaging in premarital sex, and many of them have said, "He told me he really loved me, so I gave in." Later, they discovered the guy didn't really love them—he was just interested in sex. That's selfish love. Unselfish love, on the other hand, seeks what is best for the other person. Unselfish love is patient. Unselfish love will wait.

Jesus said in Luke 6:35-38, "Help and give without expecting a return. You'll never—I promise— regret it. Live out this God-created identity the way our Father lives toward us, generously and graciously, even when we're at our worst. Our Father is kind; you be kind. Don't pick on people, jump on their failures, criticize their faults. . . . Give away your life" (THE MESSAGE).

When I traveled to India a few years ago, I visited Mother Teresa's grave. It was a very powerful experience for me. There, inscribed in stone, are Jesus' words: "Love as I have loved you." Wouldn't the world be a different place if all people looked at everyone as if they were Jesus—rather than someone to use, then discard? Others will take notice if we decide to follow Jesus' example of gentle, sacrificial, unselfish love.

Looking Further

Among other things, Paul warned Timothy that in the last days people will be "lovers of themselves, lovers of money. . . without love . . . not lovers of the good . . . lovers of pleasure rather than lovers of God" (for the complete list, see 2 Tim. 3:1-5).

In contrast to this, Paul admonishes us:

> Don't run up debts, except for the huge debt of love you owe each other. When you love others, you complete what the law has been after all along. The law code—don't sleep with another person's spouse, don't take someone's life, don't take what isn't yours, don't always be wanting what you don't have, and any other "don't" you can think of— finally adds up to this: Love other people as well as you do yourself. You can't go wrong when you love others. When you add up everything in the law code, the sum total is *love*. (Rom. 13:8-10, THE MESSAGE)

Living It Out

In all of your relationships, God calls you to love as He has loved you . . . unconditionally, unselfishly, without expecting anything in return. How will that impact your daily choices? Ask God to give you a heart of service toward everyone who crosses your path today.

DAY FIFTY-SIX

Our Security

You can go to bed without fear; you will lie down and sleep soundly. You need not be afraid of sudden disaster or the destruction that comes upon the wicked, for the LORD is your security. He will keep your foot from being caught in a trap.

—Proverbs 3:24-26, NLT

Reflection

Several years ago I spent some time with about eight hundred teenage girls in Panama before they set out on a mission trip to Quito, Ecuador. I noticed that some of the girls were dealing with appearance-related issues. Some were cutting themselves because they felt so badly about their self-image or were so emotionally shut down that they just wanted to feel something—even if it was pain. Some of them were struggling with anorexia or bulimia; some felt a lack of trust in men because they had been abused; others were struggling with homosexuality. It's easy to think that these kinds of issues happen only outside the church, but they also occur inside the church's walls.

Many of us struggle with our appearance because we've been exposed to so many false ideas of beauty and have seen so much immorality portrayed in the media. We sometimes think that what we see represented there is normal. We may feel as if we are all alone and unprotected. We all need to know that real and lasting security is found in God. We all have a basic need to be protected, cocooned in love, and sheltered from danger.

During a difficult time in my life when I felt very alone, disillusioned, and unprotected, I often cried out to God in desperation. My future looked bleak and empty. Because of what was going on in me internally, I went into a self-protection mode. I began to shut off and shut down. I shared my situation and pain with my pastor. After listening to my concerns, he said, "Rebecca, is God trustworthy?" When I answered in the affirmative, he said, "Then trust Him." Those words of wisdom were so powerful. I finally realized how much I had been relying on myself, trying to be strong and independent rather than finding my identity and protection in God.

Looking Further

When King David felt vulnerable and susceptible to various attacks from his enemies, he pictured God covering him with the shadow of His powerful wings. What a vivid image of God's shelter and strength for His loved ones!

- "Show me your unfailing love in wonderful ways. By your mighty power you rescue those who seek refuge from their enemies. Guard me as you would guard your own eyes. Hide me in the shadow of your wings" (Ps. 17:7-8, NLT).
- "How precious is your unfailing love, O God! All humanity finds shelter in the shadow of your wings" (Ps. 36:7, NLT).
- "Have mercy on me, O God, have mercy on me, for in you my soul takes refuge. I will take refuge in the shadow of your wings until the disaster has passed" (Ps. 57:1).
- "Because you are my helper, I sing for joy in the shadow of your wings. I cling to you; your strong right hand holds me securely" (Ps. 63:7-8, NLT).

Living It Out

Are there past hurts in your life that make you feel insecure about your body? How does this insecurity affect your everyday life? What makes you feel better when you sense that you are alone and unprotected? What is your biggest source of shelter in the midst of a storm? Do you believe that God can protect you? How can you make God your greatest source of security in the future?

DAY FIFTY-SEVEN

Carrying Each Other

If someone is caught in a sin, you who are spiritual should restore him gently. But watch yourself, or you also may be tempted. Carry each other's burdens, and in this way you will fulfill the law of Christ.

—Galatians 6:1-2

Reflection

It was a race, an event you didn't have to compete in to be moved by. In fact, you didn't even have to be there to get it. I watched the race from half a world away, from the comfort of my motor home while I was on tour—months after the event actually took place. The race was run in my homeland of Australia. Known as the "Eco-Challenge," it consisted of three hundred miles of nonstop kayaking, hiking, mountain biking, cliff climbing, walking, and rafting. Exhausting even to think of! The Challenge took seven to ten days, with stops only for the basic needs of survival. Organizers say that the key elements of running the race are honest communication, compassion, and focus on the mission. The goal is to endure to the end and finish the race as a team.

Challengers came from all over the world. As I watched, wanting to root wholeheartedly for my fellow Aussies, I was instead moved by what I saw unfolding. The Chinese team of three young men and one young woman captured my heart. They had been making progress through the rough Australian terrain when the nightmare began. The lone girl member injured her foot and was noticeably weakened. Still she went on, until finally, after many miles, she could go no farther. A great distance was still ahead of the team, but with one fallen member they were looking at the strong possibility of not being able to finish the race.

One of the most important rules in the Eco-Challenge is that all team members must cross the finish line together. And this is where the Chinese challenged me—sitting comfortably back in America watching their plight via video. A remarkable thing happened. Instead of quitting, the strong loaned their strength to the weak. The men took turns running ahead and resting in brief intervals so that when the team caught up, a rested member could take the female teammate from the back of another and carry her—over mountains, over rocks, running with her on their backs through every obstacle. Their tenacious commitment to finishing the race together brought tears to my eyes.

What a picture of how members of the body of Christ should care for one another. In your determination to remain pure in body, in times of weakness you may need to rely on the strength

of another team member. This person might be an accountability partner, someone who knows your weaknesses and loves
you just the same. God never intended for any of us to go it
alone. He knows that all of us, if caught alone by the enemy, are
vulnerable to temptation. But together, we are strong!

Looking Further

Philippians 3:12-14 and Hebrews 12:1 liken the Christian journey to a race, one that we must run with patience and endurance toward the prize of eternal life that is set before us. We are
called to love our brothers and sisters in the Lord so much that
we will help them cross the finish line even at very great cost to
our own lives. Jesus said in John 15:13 that there is no greater
love than when a man lays down his life for his friends. It might
take sacrifice on our part to pick someone up who is weak and
in danger of not finishing the race strong, but it is not an
option—it's our obligation as members of the same team.

Living It Out

Which of these keys to helping your teammates succeed comes
hardest for you?

- *Honest communication* (speaking into your teammates' lives with
  truth and authenticity, motivated by a desire to bring out
  the best in them)
- *Compassion* (listening and understanding, even when your
  teammates have fallen and need help standing back up)
- *Staying focused on the mission* (keeping the goal of finishing strong
  in sight)

What opportunities will you look for today to help a teammate succeed?

DAY FIFTY-EIGHT

Overcoming Bitterness

*I realized that my heart was bitter, and I was all torn up inside. I was so fool-
ish and ignorant—I must have seemed like a senseless animal to you. Yet I still
belong to you; you hold my right hand. You guide me with your counsel, leading
me to a glorious destiny.*

—Psalm 73:21-24, NLT

Reflection

One of the harshest realities I've come to see as I've met people
on tour is the large number of women and girls whose lives
have been devastated by rape. When that happens, the question
always arises, "Why did God allow this to happen to me?" In
some instances the difficulties became worse when the girl discovered she was pregnant. Imagine a Christian young woman
in this situation. She's embarrassed and afraid. Because she be-
lieves in the sanctity of all human life in God's eyes, abortion
is not an option—yet thoughts of it trouble her mind. Every
time she thinks about the baby, she remembers the horrific experience. Perhaps she feels a touch of resentment toward the
baby and much more than a touch of anger toward the one who
violated her. She may feel that because of what happened to

her, she is no longer sexually pure—even if she was not a willing participant.

I can't begin to imagine the anguish of these circumstances, but I do know that in any situation, we can either turn toward God or turn away from Him. I don't pretend to understand it, but God assures us that He can relate to all our pain and that He really does want to work through it with us to bring us closer to Himself. In any given situation, we can choose to hold on to our pain, to blame God, and not forgive those who have hurt us. But in so doing, we choose to allow a root of bitterness to grow and eventually destroy us. Every day we have the power to decide whether we will let the circumstances of life make us *bitter* or *better*.

Looking Further

When his father, Isaac, was old and could no longer see, Jacob conspired with his mother, Rebekah, to trick Isaac into giving Jacob the firstborn blessing that was due Jacob's twin brother, Esau. After quite an elaborate plan of dressing in Esau's clothes so that he would smell like him and attaching goatskin to his hands and neck so that he would feel like him (because Esau was a hairy man), Jacob's deception worked. Earlier, Jacob had traded Esau a measly bowl of lentil stew for his birthright; now Jacob also had the firstborn blessing—which could not be retracted. When Esau came in from the field and discovered what had taken place, he "burst out with a loud and bitter cry and said to his father, 'Bless me—me too, my father!'" (Gen. 27:34). But it was too late—Jacob had stolen his blessing. Esau held a grudge for quite some time and planned to kill Jacob after the death of their father. But he never carried out his plan. Eventually, the two brothers came back together, and then parted in peace.

The author of Hebrews holds up the example of Esau to point out the kind of bitterness we need to avoid:

> Work at living in peace with everyone, and work at living a holy life, for those who are not holy will not see the Lord. Look after each other so that none of you fails to receive the grace of God. Watch out that no poisonous root of bitterness grows up to trouble you, corrupting many. Make sure that no one is immoral or godless like Esau, who traded his birthright as the firstborn son for a single meal. You know that afterward, when he wanted his father's blessing, he was rejected. It was too late for repentance, even though he begged with bitter tears. (12:14-17, NLT)

If you (or someone you know) have been raped, the experience is far more hurtful than the deception that Jacob received at the hands of his brother, Esau. If you haven't already done so, please seek the professional help you need so that hope, rather than bitterness, will be your companion for life. God desires for you to be healed.

Living It Out

Are there any events in your past over which you harbor bitterness? God longs for you to let them go and turn them over to Him, knowing that if you don't, they will drag your spirit down. No matter what the situation, in His strength you *can* overcome!

DAY FIFTY-NINE

Guarding Our Hearts

End the evil of those who are wicked, and defend the righteous. For you look deep within the mind and heart, O righteous God. God is my shield, saving those whose hearts are true and right.

—Psalm 7:9-10, NLT

Reflection

One day I was talking about purity of mind, heart, and body with my Nanna, and she said this: "Television doesn't help. As soon as I see a bad movie coming on, I turn it off. Don't watch things that display immoral activity, because we learn by seeing. You might feel that you can 'handle it,' but Satan is sneaky, and he creeps in, conditioning our minds to accept wrong things. Before we know it, these things become actions in our lives." I agree with this wise woman. We must guard our hearts, because if we are not careful, what we allow to lodge in our minds can creep into our hearts and eventually come out in our actions.

It is essential that we spend time with God and ask Him to make us clean by washing us with His Word (see Eph. 5:26). We need to ask Him to shield us from the things that would damage our minds, hearts, and bodies. As we do so, the things of the world will fade into the background. And it's not enough to guard our own hearts in the area of sexual purity. We must also help guard others' hearts. We have an obligation to not wrong our brothers or sisters by taking advantage of them, because

God has called us to a holy life (see 1 Thess. 4:6-7). That means we should be concerned with the way we dress, so we don't tempt guys. It also means we are vigilant to help them remain sexually pure by not tempting them to do immoral things with us. It's a responsibility we should not take lightly, and one I believe we will be held accountable for.

Looking Further

Throughout the book of Exodus, God spoke to Moses about setting things apart for Himself. The Sabbath was to be different from any other day of the week; the tabernacle was to be set apart as His special dwelling place; and the tribe of Levi was to be specially set apart for service in the tabernacle. God chose to identify Himself during this time period as *Jehovah m'kaddesh*, which means, "The God who sanctifies," or "The God who makes holy" (see Exod. 31:12-13). In Leviticus 20:7-8, God said to Moses, "Set yourselves apart to be holy, for I am the LORD your God. Keep all my decrees by putting them into practice, for I am the LORD who makes you holy" (NLT).

As we strive to guard our hearts, minds, and bodies, we cannot do so in our own strength. It is *God* who sanctifies! His goal for our lives is that we will be holy and blameless, without stain or blemish (see Eph. 5:27). And we can achieve this holiness only through the blood of Jesus. Hebrews 10:10-12, 14 describes it in these words:

> God's will was for us to be made holy by the sacrifice of the body of Jesus Christ, once for all time. Under the old covenant, the priest stands and ministers before the altar day after day, offering the same sacrifices again and

again, which can never take away sins. But our High Priest offered himself to God as a single sacrifice for sins, good for all time. Then he sat down in the place of honor at God's right hand. . . . For by that one offering he forever made perfect those who are being made holy. (NLT)

Living It Out Thankfully! — I praise you, Father!

God is making you holy. It is a lifelong process. You'll never achieve perfection this side of heaven, but because of what Jesus has done for you on the cross, you can stand out and be distinctive. Ask God to give you the strength to be different from the rest of the world.

Day Sixty

Carrying the Message with You

Go out into the world uncorrupted, a breath of fresh air in this squalid and polluted society. Provide people with a glimpse of good living and of the living God. Carry the light-giving Message into the night so I'll have good cause to be proud of you on the day that Christ returns.

—Philippians 2:15-16, The Message

Reflection

I've had the privilege of seeing God on the move in Europe. In places like Holland, Norway, and England, audiences receive the encouragement that comes from Christian music with such a fresh enthusiasm and joy. Whenever I travel to Europe I'm excited to see what God will do through me. Proverbs 11:25 says, "He who refreshes others will himself be refreshed." That's really true. I am always refreshed by being with my brothers and sisters in these parts of the world.

One time I took a midnight tour of Red Square in Moscow and posed in front of the light-bathed Kremlin. Russia was truly an incredible experience! From the bouquet of roses I received at the airport to the tremendously warm reception I received at the concert, God moved in Moscow, and it was such a wonderful experience to be a part of what He was doing.

I was blessed to be able to bring God's message to parts of Europe—many of them formerly Communist countries—that few Christian artists have been able to see. God is alive and on the move in such places as the former Soviet Union, Germany, the Netherlands, Hungary, Estonia, Austria, and Bulgaria. I saw some incredible acts of God—but also some profound pockets of darkness throughout my European travels. It made me want to go back—and encourage others to take up the challenge as well.

As you stand for purity, God will use you to carry this message to others who need to hear it. We live in a very dark world, but there are people all around you at home, at church, and at work who are looking for others who are willing to stand out and be different. You never know when your example will be exactly what another man or woman desperately needs to see. . . . You are proof that it's possible to live a pure life in this dark and perverted world!

Looking Further

Acts 1:8 tells us that just before Jesus ascended back to heaven, He promised His disciples they would receive power from the Holy Spirit that would enable them to tell people everywhere about the good news of the gospel . . . "in Jerusalem, throughout Judea, in Samaria, and to the ends of the earth" (NLT). Acts 2 records the events that transpired as the disciples began to share the truth about Jesus' death, burial, and resurrection in their immediate surroundings (Jerusalem). Then the remainder of the book of Acts tells of the expansion of their mission. Simon Peter labored all the way to Rome, where he was eventually martyred. According to the historian Eusebius, Simon's brother Andrew preached in Scythia, located between the Black and Caspian seas. Some traditions claim that Bartholomew preached as far as Ethiopia or Arabia, while Thomas may have traveled as far as India. Because of all the wonders they had personally seen Jesus do, His disciples were sold out to proclaiming the good news of His salvation as far as God allowed them to go—no matter what the cost.

Living It Out

Just as Jesus challenged His disciples, He is calling you to step out in faith beginning with where you live (*your* Jerusalem), then moving on to your Judea, Samaria, and possibly the ends of the earth. You may never get the chance to carry the gospel of Jesus to Europe, but then again, you just might. Opportunities to stand for purity and God's truth are all around you. What will you do today?

PURITY OF SPIRIT

Day Sixty-one

Hearing from God

The one who enters through the gate is the shepherd of the sheep. The gate-keeper opens the gate for him, and the sheep recognize his voice and come to him. He calls his own sheep by name and leads them out. After he has gathered his own flock, he walks ahead of them, and they follow him because they know his voice.

—John 10:2-4, NLT

Reflection

Like everyone else, I experience seasons when it's tough to stay consistent in my time with God, seeking Him whether I feel like it or not. There are days when it's not convenient to stop everything and have devotional time with God, but I know how important it is. I know that unless I seek Him daily, I'm not going to be filled up, I'm not going to have anything to give to others, and I'll be going backward in my walk with Him—which I definitely don't want. At times when I need a kick start in my faith, I read books by Christian authors whom I respect, seek wisdom by talking with my pastor, and ask others to pray for me—that God will put a fresh word in my heart.

Our Father greatly desires to communicate with His children in intimate ways. God speaks to those He loves in a variety of ways. Often He speaks to me through His Word in the Bible, as well as in everyday practical ways in my life. I often pray that I'll be sensitive to His will. The morning I was leaving for my trip overseas to L'Abri, I got up extra early to take a walk in my garden. It was very misty; then suddenly the sun arose on the horizon. God spoke to my heart and said, "Rebecca, I have a new sunrise like that coming into your life." I can't remember that moment without smiling. His promise proved to be true—the journey that lay ahead of me that morning was all He promised it would be—a new sunrise.

When we pray, God wants us to be still and quiet so that we can clearly hear from Him. When we're in a real spirit of prayer, we humble ourselves before Him, proclaiming, "God, I need You, and I can't do this thing called life without You." Prayer changes things, and it certainly changes us!

When we pray for purity in our spirits, we are asking God to tune us in to His purpose for our lives. We truly desire to hear from Him. We want to talk with Him as our loving heavenly Father and be assured that He is listening. We long to hear His gentle voice and know that He has taken notice and that He cares.

Looking Further

It must have been completely mind-blowing to see Moses when he came down from being with God on His mountain for forty days. Exodus records these words:

> When Moses came down from Mount Sinai with the two tablets of the Testimony in his hands, he was not aware that his face was radiant because he had spoken with the LORD. When Aaron and all the Israelites saw Moses, his face was radiant, and they were afraid to come near him. But Moses called to them; so Aaron and all the leaders

of the community came back to him, and he spoke to them. Afterward all the Israelites came near him, and he gave them all the commands the LORD had given him on Mount Sinai.

When Moses finished speaking to them, he put a veil over his face. But whenever he entered the LORD's presence to speak with him, he removed the veil until he came out. And when he came out and told the Israelites what he had been commanded, they saw that his face was radiant. Then Moses would put the veil back over his face until he went in to speak with the LORD. (4:29-35)

Moses' face was radiant because he had spent prolonged and intense time with God. You may never have that kind of sunburn from being with God, but it is possible for people to know that you have spent time with Him by the countenance they see on your face and the attitude they see expressed by your spirit.

Living It Out

How do you best hear God's will for your life? How does He reveal the purity you are to have in your spirit? Through His Word? Extended alone time with Him? The godly counsel of others in your life who know Him intimately? Make time today to listen to His voice.

Books (Bible, fiction, nonfiction)
Writing (journaling, poetry, memoir)
Prayer (journaling, spoken + unspoken)
Company (family, friends, colleagues)
Running/Alone time

DAY SIXTY-TWO

A Submissive Spirit

During the days of Jesus' life on earth, he offered up prayers and petitions with loud cries and tears to the one who could save him from death, and he was heard because of his reverent submission. Although he was a son, he learned obedience from what he suffered and, once made perfect, he became the source of eternal salvation for all who obey him.

—Hebrews 5:7-9

Reflection

When I was in Romania, I worked at a girls' home, and their leader's name was Catalin. A few of us workers were coming back in Catalin's car one day, and as we rode we noticed that one of his car windows had been broken and would have to be replaced. We helped him carry the plates of glass into the house. I asked him, "Where do you want us to put them?" He said to put them in the hallway (which had a tile floor). I thought it might be a bit dangerous because there were children around. I put the glass in a different room, one that was carpeted. Catalin told me that I would have to work on that when I was married. It was a little thing, but it wasn't really my place to make that decision. I had the opportunity to practice submission—and I chose my own way.

In today's world, *submission* seems to be a dirty word. Most people would rather be in charge and make their own decisions than submit to the wishes of others—whether that's at home or on the job. Willful submission is not held in very high regard in popular culture. As a matter of fact, it is generally seen as a sign of weakness. You never hear it talked about in Hollywood marriages. More people seem to be concerned with standing up for their rights than laying them down for others. One of the things that can distinctly set believers apart from the rest of the world is an attitude of humble submission in deference to others. Jesus is the ultimate example of this. And we would be wise to follow.

Looking Further

Throughout the Bible we are commanded to submit our will to others'. God expects us to submit . . .

- *to Himself*—"Submit to God and be at peace with him; in this way prosperity will come to you" (Job 22:21); "Since we respected our earthly fathers who disciplined us, shouldn't we submit even more to the discipline of the Father of our spirits, and live forever?" (Heb. 12:9, NLT).
- *to our parents*—"It is good for people to submit at an early age to the yoke of his discipline" (Lam. 3:27, NLT).
- *to the government*—"Remind the believers to submit to the government and its officers. They should be obedient, always ready to do what is good" (Titus 3:1, NLT).
- *to our spouses*—"Submit to one another out of reverence for Christ. Wives, submit to your husbands as to the Lord" (Eph. 5:21-22). Colossians 3:18 and Titus 2:5 also command wives to submit to their husbands.

Living It Out

The commands are pretty clear. The only question is, will we choose to obey them? Submitting to others' wishes definitely goes against the grain of the world's ways. But God's way is always better—and it always works. In which of the above categories do you have the hardest time exhibiting a submissive spirit? With Jesus as your example, make a determined effort today to walk in submission.

DAY SIXTY-THREE

God, Help Me

I call to God; GOD will help me. At dusk, dawn, and noon I sigh deep sighs—he hears, he rescues. My life is well and whole, secure in the middle of danger even while thousands are lined up against me.

—Psalm 55:16-18, THE MESSAGE

Reflection

One of the ways in which God purifies our spirits is by allowing us to go through struggles. As Christians we may sometimes feel that we're supposed to have it all together, that we shouldn't struggle. But when we experience difficulty, it's okay to cry out, "God, help me. I'm hurting," just as the people of the Bible did.

In Psalm 109:26, David wrote, "Help me, O LORD my God; save me in accordance with your love." We all go through times when we feel alone or afraid, moments when the circumstances we're in pierce us with doubt and uncertainty. Those times call for faith on our part. Faith wouldn't be faith without having to trust what is unseen. Sometimes it's easier to put our trust in what is seen, what is tangible. But God wants us to put one foot in front of the other and just step out in faith.

And when we truly do that, we will begin to see Him working in our lives in very active ways. But we've got to look for His provision. His answers are not going to just pop up right in front of us in 3-D because that wouldn't take very much faith. God is calling us to completely and fully trust in Him as the God of our future. We can trust that He has an amazing plan for our lives and He is going to take care of us.

God understands our trials. He wants us to turn to Him and share everything we are going through. God is always there for us to call upon. He's our refuge and strength, our ever-present help in times of trouble. Whether we sing out to Him with our praises or cry out to Him in our weaknesses and tears, He is always there to meet us, even through the simplest heart cry: "God, help me!"

Looking Further

A brief scanning of the Psalms reveals that King David, who penned many of them, was constantly in danger from enemies or even family members. His list of pursuers included the barbaric Philistines, King Saul, Abimelech, and his rebellious son Absalom. That's why David's words as he hid for protection are filled with heart cries to God for help, and why many people turn to the book of Psalms when they feel as if the world is closing in on them.

Perhaps you can identify with some of David's feelings in these words:

✓ "The LORD hears his people when they call to him for help. He rescues them from all their troubles. The LORD is close to the brokenhearted; he rescues those whose spirits are crushed. The righteous person faces many troubles, but the LORD comes to the rescue each time" (Ps. 34:17-19, NLT).

✓ "Hear my cry, O God; listen to my prayer. From the ends of the earth I call to you, I call as my heart grows faint; lead me to the rock that is higher than I. For you have been my refuge, a strong tower against the foe" (Ps. 61:1-3).

Living It Out

When you're in the midst of a tough time, do you seek God's face for a solution as the first resort—or the last? Do you sometimes think the small things are too trivial to bring to Him, and approach Him only with the real biggies? Because He cares so desperately for you, He wants you to bring them all—big and small—and lay them at His feet. What's preventing you from doing that today? He's waiting.

DAY SIXTY-FOUR

Fighting Through the Tough Times

Consider it a sheer gift, friends, when tests and challenges come at you from all sides. You know that under pressure, your faith-life is forced into the open and shows its true colors. . . . Anyone who meets a testing challenge head-on and manages to stick it out is mighty fortunate. For such persons loyally in love with God, the reward is life and more life.

—James 1:2-3, 12, THE MESSAGE

Reflection

If you've been a Christian for any length of time, you have undoubtedly experienced seasons of weariness in trying to stay on the straight and narrow path. In our quest for living a pure, focused life that pleases God, we all hit the wall at one time or another. What do we do then? Give up and decide it's no longer any use to keep trying? Not an option. I have times when the road gets long and I miss home and find myself yearning for normal life and my friends. Those periods can be very challenging. When they happen, I go to God and ask for His strength for the journey.

One of the benefits of getting through the difficult moments is that when we come out on the other side, we have grown through the adversity in ways we would not have grown otherwise. And when more than our power and strength has been required to make it on our own, we know beyond certainty that it was God, and not ourselves, that got us through. He receives greater glory when we are depleted and cry out to Him for the strength to walk through the hardship.

I have found that another key to survival is to lean on the community of faith God has given me. In recent years I have discovered more about the power of community by being honest and asking friends to walk with me through the lonely and difficult times. Sometimes just asking for prayer or chatting on the phone helps immensely. I now understand the power of being vulnerable and open within safe friendships. That's empowering. Knowing God is using my life and ministry also definitely helps encourage me through any hard times. And God is using your life and ministry too as you walk closely with Him.

Looking Further

It's been said, "Tough times don't last; tough people do." The following verses are all taken from *The Message*, which is a modern paraphrase of the Bible written by Eugene Peterson. I love what these verses say about hanging tough when we feel like throwing in the towel.

- "GOD is good, a hiding place in tough times. He recognizes and welcomes anyone looking for help, no matter how desperate the trouble" (Nah. 1:7-8).
- [Paul and Barnabas urged the disciples] "to stick with what they had begun to believe and not quit, making it clear to them that it wouldn't be easy: 'Anyone signing up for the kingdom of God has to go through plenty of hard times'" (Acts 14:22).
- "Don't burn out; keep yourselves fueled and aflame. Be

alert servants of the Master, cheerfully expectant. Don't quit in hard times; pray all the harder" (Rom. 12:11-12).

"He comes alongside us when we go through hard times, and before you know it, he brings us alongside someone else who is going through hard times so that we can be there for that person just as God was there for us. We have plenty of hard times that come from following the Messiah, but no more so than the good times of his healing comfort—we get a full measure of that, too" (2 Cor. 1:4-5).

"We're not giving up. How could we! Even though on the outside it often looks like things are falling apart on us, on the inside, where God is making new life, not a day goes by without his unfolding grace. These hard times are small potatoes compared to the coming good times, the lavish celebration prepared for us" (2 Cor. 4:16-17).

Living It Out

The next time you face a difficult situation (maybe even today), pull out the above verses and meditate on them. God is always faithful to fulfill the promises in His Word. That's a truth you can rely on.

DAY SIXTY-FIVE

We Are Weak, but He Is Strong

He told me, "My grace is enough; it's all you need. My strength comes into its own in your weakness." Once I heard that, I was glad to let it happen. I quit focusing on the handicap and began appreciating the gift. It was a case of Christ's strength moving in on my weakness. Now I take limitations in stride, and with good cheer, these limitations that cut me down to size—abuse, accidents, opposition, bad breaks. I just let Christ take over! And so the weaker I get, the stronger I become.

—2 Corinthians 12:9-10, THE MESSAGE

Reflection

Have you ever heard the saying "Everything I need to know in life, I learned in kindergarten"? Many of us learned a great deal in Sunday school, singing in our best and most earnest voices the words to "Jesus Loves Me": "Little ones to Him belong, they are weak, but He is strong!" We all face times in life when we find that we, in our humanness, are not sufficient for the task at hand. That's when we also have the opportunity to discover firsthand that in our weakness, God is strong.

I once participated in an event called *Thrive* that was telecast live via closed circuit to churches across the country. I was not feeling very well the day of my concert—physically, emotionally, and spiritually I felt quite vulnerable. I was also a little nervous about sharing the stage with the other women at the event—women such as Kay Arthur, Liz Curtis Higgs, and Lynne

Hybels. If there was ever a time I wanted to feel I was "game on" musically and every other way, it was then—and I wasn't feeling that way at all. I spoke with a friend right before I went onstage and asked her to pray for me.

She said, "Rebecca, I want you to remember what it means to be a jar of clay. Even if we have only a few drops left in the bottom of the jar—that's a good thing! It allows God to fill us up rather than our being filled up in our own strength. I want to encourage you to go out there knowing that God can use you probably more effectively in your weakness than He could if you were feeling strong today."

Her encouragement changed my whole outlook so much that day. It gave me an instant spiritual transformation. My spirit just felt so much lighter and free. I was able to share honestly with the audience about how there needs to be a place for honesty and vulnerability within our relationships. That openness promotes community and an atmosphere where we can then turn to God together. What a powerful and beautiful thing that is.

Looking Further

Some people think they can handle everything on their own, as if they are islands unto themselves, but sooner or later they will run into a situation in which they must draw on strength from outside themselves. It might be a serious health issue, a financial burden, a difficult decision that must be made, or the need to overcome a nagging sin. How terrible it must be for the person who feels as if she has nowhere to turn to in those difficult times. God has provided strength for your life not only through His own supernatural power but also through the friends He has brought into your path. The Christian life

Carol

can be lived properly only in community—walking in intimacy with the Father and doing life together with faithful brothers and sisters in the kingdom of God.

The wise man Solomon said in Ecclesiastes 4:12, "By yourself you're unprotected. With a friend you can face the worst. Can you round up a third? A three-stranded rope isn't easily snapped" (THE MESSAGE).

Living It Out

Is there an area in your life right now in which you feel particularly weak and vulnerable? Be straight with those who are closest to you about what's going on in your life, and you'll find strength in God and in the community He's surrounded you with. Take heart, help is on the way.

DAY SIXTY-SIX

Mirror, Mirror on the Wall

Charm can mislead and beauty soon fades. The woman to be admired and praised is the woman who lives in the Fear-of-GOD. Give her everything she deserves! Festoon her life with praises!

—Proverbs 31:30-31, THE MESSAGE

Reflection

So many women I have met believe the culture's lies regarding feminism and beauty. The feminist movement freed women in some ways but put them in bondage in others. The enemy would have us believe that what we see on television and in magazines defines real femininity and beauty. But it's all really a facade. Many glamorous actresses and models are extremely unhappy. Almost daily we hear of another celebrity's battle with alcohol or drug abuse or eating disorders—all results of buying into the enemy's agenda.

We've got to get our ideas of true femininity and beauty from God. That is the only thing that can free us from the bondage of the enemy's lies. Only by seeking God can we truly experience intimacy with Him and others and understand our God-given purpose. We need what I call a "new feminism," which says, "If the old feminism was about freedom for women to be all that they can be, this is about freedom for women to be *in God* all that they can be." We are called to be true women of God and to live the fullest life possible—as He designed us to be and to do!

The Bible was way ahead of us in exposing the cultural beauty myth for what it is. The next time you look in the mirror, picture God looking over your shoulder. Even though the original intent of some of these verses was directed to a prophet or to God's people, Israel, in the larger sense these passages express God's heart for you. Here's what He has to say about you:

- *You are beautiful:* "You grew up and became a beautiful jewel" (Ezek. 16:7, NLT).
- *You are treasured:* "The LORD your God has chosen you to be his own special treasure" (Deut. 7:6, NLT).
- *You are precious:* "You are very precious to God" (Dan. 10:19, NLT).
- *You are honored:* "You are precious to me. You are honored, and I love you" (Isa. 43:4, NLT).
- *You are one of a kind:* "I knew you before I formed you in your mother's womb. Before you were born I set you apart" (Jer. 1:5, NLT).
- *You are loved:* "He loves us with unfailing love" (Ps. 117:2, NLT).

Looking Further

God has created very beautiful things and people, but He is really into inner beauty and purity of spirit. Man looks at the outward appearance, but God looks at the heart. The apostle Peter said it like this: "Don't be concerned about the outward beauty of fancy hairstyles, expensive jewelry, or beautiful clothes. You should clothe yourselves instead with the beauty that comes from within, the unfading beauty of a gentle and quiet spirit, which is so precious to God. This is how the holy women of old made themselves beautiful" (1 Pet. 3:3-5, NLT).

Paul told Timothy, "I want women to get in there with the men in humility before God, not primping before a mirror or chasing the latest fashions but doing something beautiful for God and becoming beautiful doing it" (1 Tim. 2:9-10, THE MESSAGE).

Looking in the mirror isn't bad, and there's certainly nothing wrong with wanting to look your best—but seeing the inner mirror of your spirit is what really counts before God.

Living It Out

Every time someone in your life (or that inner voice) prompts a whispered statement in your mind such as, *"You are unlovely," "You are ugly," "You are fat,"* or *"You are not capable,"* speak aloud one of God's true "You are" statements. That is the truth that will set you free! Walk in that assurance today as you live the beautiful life God intended you to live.

DAY SIXTY-SEVEN

Relying on the Spirit

Don't worry about what you'll say. When the time comes, say what's on your heart—the Holy Spirit will make his witness in and through you.

—Mark 13:11, THE MESSAGE

Reflection

I was fifteen years old when I signed my first contract in the music industry. Many people wondered if I had anything to say to other teens and adults, and at times I've wondered the very same thing! Prayer has always been a big part of my ministry. Often I've come to God and said, "Lord, I don't know what to say in this situation—fill my mouth!" During many of my tours, I have an interview section in the middle of the concert in which the audience can ask any questions they desire. While the questions are being asked, I often pray, "Lord, give me the words to say." Just giving it over to God for His inspiration has gotten me through some pretty hard questions. For a teenage girl that was pretty intimidating stuff, but God always gave me words that I knew could have come only from the Holy Spirit's leading.

I once had the opportunity to be on the *Hannity & Colmes* TV show on Valentine's Day. I especially felt the Holy Spirit leading and guiding me that day. The telecast consisted of a discussion in which a well-known sex therapist and I debated the question, "Should people save sex for marriage?" The producers of the show were hoping it would create an entertaining debate. I was on tour with the Newsboys during that time, and in one of the concerts leading up to the TV show, a concert promoter hosting the event asked the audience to pray for me—that the Holy Spirit would inspire me. I so saw God answer that prayer!

Right before I went on air via satellite (for about ten or fifteen minutes leading up to the telecast), I felt God giving me certain points to make in relation to the issue of saving sex for marriage—things I had never thought about in ten years of speaking on the subject. I jotted down some notes, hoping I would have a chance to share them during the debate. You never know what direction an interview might take, so it's a miracle to me that I was able to use every single thought I had written down. God had totally and perfectly prepared me for that interview. For example, one of the points the sex therapist made was this: "I believe you need to have sex before marriage to find out if you're sexually compatible." Prior to going on air, God had given me this to say: "I am so much more than just a sexual being—I don't want someone to choose to marry me based on my sexual performance."

God revealed His hand in a practical way through the inspiration of the Holy Spirit. It was a very affirming time in my ministry and in my personal walk with God. And I'm confident God will reveal Himself in personal ways to anyone who chooses to walk closely with Him.

Looking Further

In John 16, Jesus promised that He would send His Holy Spirit to guide His believers into all truth. If we sincerely approach God in faith, seeking His perspective on an issue, He will do what He promised—reveal His truth to us. But when we do so, we must make a commitment to come with a singular focus, believing that what He says is the only word we need to hear (see James 1:5-8).

Living It Out

Do you want to know God's heart on a particular dilemma you're facing right now? You can try to figure it out on your own, pool the opinions of others in your life, or go to the real source, asking God's Spirit to reveal His perfect will. He loves it when we come to Him in search of truth, and He will answer us when we call.

Day Sixty-eight

Heaven on Earth

May your Kingdom come soon. May your will be done on earth, as it is in heaven.

—Matthew 6:10, NLT

Reflection

This past year my study group read the book *Simply Christian: Why Christianity Makes Sense*, by N. T. Wright.[14] I really enjoyed the way much of his thinking stretched me. Wright wrote that "the church should awaken its hunger for beauty at every level." I have adopted that goal. I desire to beautify the world as best I can, whether through cleaning my house, having an inspiring conversation with someone, or serving in a way that makes another feel loved. These are all ways in which I can beautify the world around me.

A few years ago, I returned to Oberhofen, Austria, to do a concert with Father Christoph and the wonderful people there. Reflecting on the experience, Father said, "It was one of the most important days of my life because it was evident that the Lord is using different people for His service in one spirit working together. I don't like loud music, and I am a fan of Mozart, but the Lord showed me that other sorts of music can make a difference, and His Holy Spirit was at work yesterday. At the concert, we felt such an atmosphere of openheartedness." We can, by the way in which we live, be a part of heaven beginning here on earth.

We encourage this collision of heaven and earth by simply being about the business of following Jesus—and His model for us in Scripture—as closely as possible. Our love for God and our obedience to Him are tied together in a profound way. Take one away from the other, and one's walk with God is crippled. Additionally, we are strengthened in our walk not only through our personal relationship with God but also by the ways He is working in others' lives.

There are times when someone else says exactly what I'm experiencing. In those moments, it is refreshing to know that God works in us as a community of believers. As a songwriter, I am very used to finding my own way of expressing my heart for God, but I now believe that there is value in using liturgy from others to draw near to Him in fresh ways. Whether through communing with God in prayer and in His Word, or through living in community with others, beauty is all around us.

Looking Further

David declared,

> One thing I ask of the LORD, this is what I seek: that I may
> dwell in the house of the LORD all the days of my life, to
> gaze upon the beauty of the LORD and to seek him in his
> temple. (Ps. 27:4)

Someday we won't see God's beauty just expressed through
the community we find through fellow Christians on earth.
We'll behold His beauty up close forever. John describes our
heavenly dwelling and the Lord's majesty in this way:

> I saw no temple in the city, for the Lord God Almighty
> and the Lamb are its temple. And the city has no need of
> sun or moon, for the glory of God illuminates the city,
> and the Lamb is its light. The nations will walk in its light,
> and the kings of the world will enter the city in all their
> glory. (Rev. 21:22-24, NLT)

Living It Out

In what ways do you best experience God's beauty around you?
How can you hunger to experience more of His beauty? How
can you be an active part of expressing His beauty to others?

DAY SIXTY-NINE

Take It Easy

GOD, the Master, The Holy of Israel, has this solemn counsel: "Your salvation requires you to turn back to me and stop your silly efforts to save yourselves. Your strength will come from settling down in complete dependence on me—the very thing you've been unwilling to do. . . . But GOD's not finished. He's waiting around to be gracious to you. He's gathering strength to show mercy to you. GOD takes the time to do everything right—everything. Those who wait around for him are the lucky ones."

—Isaiah 30:15, 18, THE MESSAGE

Reflection — yes! — Yes! — Yes, Yes, Yes!

Are you tired? Is your spirit weary? Do you ever just want the train to slow down so you can get off? We live in a fast-paced culture in which many people think they have to be *going* and *doing* all the time. We're used to having whatever we want right at our fingertips in an instant . . . an instant message, a download on the Internet, a book from Amazon. We even get impatient if we have to wait in the drive-through at a restaurant. In His Word, God has a lot to say about waiting. And I've learned that when I worry or get really stressed, it's because I've tried to take things into my own hands rather than relaxing and waiting on Him.

I love it when I get to go back to Australia and just chill. I visit my grandparents, cousins, and old friends. I sometimes stay in a house on the beach. I read. I pray. I swim. I study my Bible. I sit looking out onto the horizon and watch the waves.

I ride horses and go on all-day bike rides in the rain. I sleep. The time I spend in solitude with God results in an amazing refreshment and spiritual restoration. During those times, God teaches me the art of just *being* and not having to *do* anything. It is a beautiful fulfillment of the meaning of one of my favorite Scriptures, Psalm 46:10: "Be still, and know that I am God."

When we take time out to just chill and rest in God's presence, God often reveals His truths to us in new ways. When we are still long enough to actually listen, we are able to hear His will for our lives. It is through our time of resting that we build our relationship with God and prepare to see Him work in powerful ways.

Looking Further

The Hebrew word *qavah* can mean to "bind together, to gather together, to expect, to look, to wait on."[15] It is not just a twiddling-your-thumbs kind of waiting; it is an active waiting, anticipating that God is about to do something incredible. The word *qavah* . . .

- is used in reference to waiting for deliverance from one's enemies in such passages as Psalms 27:14; 69:1-6; Isaiah 49:22-23; Micah 7:6-8.
- refers to God's constant source of help in Psalms 40:1-3; 62:1, 5-8; Isaiah 30:18; 40:28-31.
- anticipates the salvation of God's righteous ones in Psalm 37:7-9; Isaiah 25:6-9; Lamentations 3:22-26.

The results of this kind of waiting are absolutely worth waiting for!

Living It Out

So, what about it? Do you need to take some extended time to get away and be with the Lord? If you can't afford to take time off, think about having some "mini-moments." Take a walk on your lunch hour; walk your pet at night; curl up in a comfy chair with your Bible, a journal, and a pen; get out some watercolor paints, put on some soothing music, and see what God allows you to create. God created the world in six days, and then He rested. What can He do while you rest in Him?

DAY SEVENTY

Beautiful Stranger

The King will say, "I'm telling the solemn truth: Whenever you did one of these things to someone overlooked or ignored, that was me—you did it to me."
—Matthew 25:40, THE MESSAGE

Reflection

Ever since I was a little girl and wanted to help kids in need by working in an orphanage, I've had a passion to show God's love to others in practical ways. I wrote the song "Beautiful Stranger" as a call to action. Every time I sing this song in concert I am personally challenged. We all encounter people in our day-to-day lives who are hurting. Rather than ignore their cries, God calls us to offer His help and hope to those who are struggling with all kinds of needs—from poverty to loneliness—and to give to those who are lost and unnoticed in the crowd.

One of the ways I've been able to express my love to Jesus is through the child sponsorship program of Compassion International, one of the world's largest Christian child development organizations. Not too long ago I got to go to Rwanda, East Africa, and meet twelve-year-old Sam, the boy I sponsor there. About twelve years ago this country was devastated by genocide. I've witnessed some of the pain of these people, but also the incredible ways in which God is pouring His love into so many people there. The highlight for me took place when I was sitting in Sam's house, asking him questions through his translator as he gently started patting my head. Meeting Sam was a life-changing experience.

My involvement with Compassion has shown me that one person really can make a difference in the fight against poverty by reaching out to an individual child. Because of my sponsorship, Sam's life will never be the same. The needs of Sam and thousands like him all over the world are being taken care of—physically, spiritually, and emotionally. Sending support through organizations is very valuable, but coupling that with physically going ourselves is really key. You could do anything, from sponsoring children to supporting ministries and organizations to going to places like Mexico, Africa, or even somewhere in your own hometown. Hands-on help is so valuable. God longs for us to respond.

Looking Further

In His parable of the sheep and the goats in Matthew 25:31-46, Jesus makes it absolutely clear that we should view people in need as if we are looking at Him. When we love someone, we are actually loving Jesus. When we stand before God, what are we going to say when He asks: "Did you feed the poor? When you saw Me hungry and thirsty, did you feed Me, and did you give Me something to drink, and did you give Me clothes?" When we love God well, the natural outflow is to love others well too.

Living It Out

Look for opportunities to go and touch the "Jesus" you see around you with your hope and love. For information about sponsoring a child, contact Compassion online at http://www.compassion.com or by calling 1-800-336-7676. What will you do to love Jesus in the flesh today?

DAY SEVENTY-ONE

A No-Revenge Policy

Don't secretly hate your neighbor. If you have something against him, get it out into the open; otherwise you are an accomplice in his guilt. Don't seek revenge or carry a grudge against any of your people. Love your neighbor as yourself. I am GOD.

—Leviticus 19:17-18, THE MESSAGE

Reflection

During a one-hundred-day campaign in 1994, Hutu extremists in Rwanda massacred an estimated eight hundred thousand people—almost one-tenth of the East African nation's population. A number of years later, I visited this nation with my younger brother Josh. We toured a genocide memorial that had been a church before the killing started. Bullet holes are still visible through the roof, and bloodstains can be seen on the walls and on a cloth at the altar. I could just barely begin to understand the profound agony of what these people had been through. What I didn't anticipate was to be humbled by the amazing beauty of forgiveness being acted out in a country that had been devastated in such a horrible way.

Rwandan president Paul Kagame instituted an official "no revenge" policy that forbade relatives of genocide victims from retaliating for atrocities done against them. Instead, they were to forgive. Whenever I share this story of the forgiveness taking place in that land, people are greatly impacted by the healing

God is bringing about there. The reason there is so much healing in that country in such a short period of time is because of
the power of forgiveness.

There is no greater example of powerful forgiveness than
Jesus' suffering and death. First Peter 2:23 says, "He did not
retaliate when he was insulted, nor threaten revenge when he
suffered. He left his case in the hands of God, who always judges
fairly" (NLT). And even as His enemies were nailing Him to the
cross and dividing His clothes among them, Jesus cried out to
God, "Father, forgive them, for they do not know what they are
doing" (Luke 23:34).

Looking Further

There is a very troubling passage found in Hebrews 10:26-31:

> Dear friends, if we deliberately continue sinning after we
> have received knowledge of the truth, there is no longer
> any sacrifice that will cover these sins. There is only the
> terrible expectation of God's judgment and the raging fire
> that will consume his enemies. For anyone who refused
> to obey the law of Moses was put to death without mercy
> on the testimony of two or three witnesses. Just think how
> much worse the punishment will be for those who have
> trampled on the Son of God, and have treated the blood
> of the covenant, which made us holy, as if it were common
> and unholy, and have insulted and disdained the Holy
> Spirit who brings God's mercy to us. For we know the one
> who said, "I will take revenge. I will pay them back." He
> also said, "The Lord will judge his own people." It is a ter-
> rible thing to fall into the hands of the living God. (NLT)

We like to meditate on God's goodness and love, but we don't want to hear much about His wrath. There are times when God says, "Enough is enough." He is extremely patient and slow to anger, but in the Old Testament, there were occasions when He took revenge on His enemies for crimes committed against Him and His chosen people (see Deut. 32:41, 43; Nah. 1:2). In His absolute justice and holiness, God certainly has the right to take revenge, but we do not (see Rom. 12:19). We are called to love our enemies regardless of what they have done (see Matt. 5:38-45).

Living It Out

Spend some time today praising God that He has instituted the ultimate "no revenge" policy for your sins. Is there someone in your life to whom you need to reach out with a no-revenge policy? In the power of God's strength, you can do it.

DAY SEVENTY-TWO

Giving Him All You've Got

When someone has been given much, much will be required in return; and when someone has been entrusted with much, even more will be required.

—Luke 12:48, NLT

Reflection

God calls us to use whatever talents He's provided in order to expand His kingdom. If you'll use the abilities He's given you for His glory, He promises to give you even more. I've seen this demonstrated many times in my life when I've found myself doing something I never would have dreamed of doing. Often when I looked back on the experience I knew it was totally a God thing. When I moved into my new home, I loved spending time doing new things—learning more about interior decorating, how to hang curtains, conquering new recipes, biking, and gardening. God is so good about providing opportunities for us to explore new hobbies and pursuits. We can view all of these interests as ways in which we can glorify Him, by delighting in the abilities He's given us and by using them to serve others too.

I do not feel worthy of being entrusted with most of the opportunities God has given me. I ask Him, "God, do You really trust me with that?" There are so many better singers and speakers and writers. When I started in ministry at such a young age, I had a lot of insecurities, and they still creep up now and then. As a member of the presidential prayer team, I had the

Yeah, there are better teachers than me

privilege of being the spokesperson for the National Day of Prayer. I never would have dreamed that I'd get to sing at the White House! I've had the opportunity to travel to numerous countries located on five different continents, and have seen some of the most beautiful sights in the world.

God has entrusted us with carrying His good news to others through a variety of means. He wants us to creatively use the talents He has blessed us with in order to share the story of His Son, Jesus, with all who will listen. The message is always the same, but the means of delivery might differ from person to person, depending on the unique giftings God has placed within us. Being trusted with this task is both exciting and scary. But it is absolutely rewarding.

Looking Further

There's an old saying that is appropriate for today: "Use it or lose it." That was certainly true in Jesus' parable of the talents recorded in Matthew 25. In one of His last parables before His death on the cross, Jesus talked about a man entrusting his property to three servants and then going on a journey. He gave a certain amount of money to each of his servants, according to each man's ability. When the master returned from his trip, he was pleased that the first two servants had each doubled the amount given to them by making wise investments. But when he discovered that out of fear the last servant did nothing but hide the money—not wanting to lose it—the master was furious, and he responded:

> That's a terrible way to live! It's criminal to live cautiously like that! If you knew I was after the best, why did you do

less than the least? The least you could have done would have been to invest the sum with the bankers, where at least I would have gotten a little interest. (Matt. 25:26-27, THE MESSAGE)

The servant's fear of losing the talent was the very thing that caused him to lose it. The master took the talent away from the lazy servant and gave it to the servant who had gained the most return on investment, then threw the worthless servant outside into the darkness. The point of the parable is this: We must ready ourselves for the return of our Master, Jesus, by taking what He's entrusted us with and producing results rather than simply coasting along and playing it safe.

Living It Out

When others talk about your talents, what do they say? Are you using those skills to accomplish God's purposes or to further your own agenda? How have you felt God tugging at your heart to use a particular talent to spread His good news? Surrender your talents and abilities to God today by asking Him to take your efforts and accomplish more than you ever would have dreamed of.

DAY SEVENTY-THREE

The Key to Aliveness

If you try to hang on to your life, you will lose it. But if you give up your life for my sake, you will save it.

—Matthew 16:25, NLT

Reflection

When we seek God's ways, striving for purity in our spirits, there is an aliveness we can experience that defies ordinary life. A couple of years ago, God used a study center in Switzerland called L'Abri to refresh and renew me. He did an amazing amount of what I like to call "heart makeover." While I was there, God did so much to revitalize and reenergize me. I realized more than ever that I want to feel really alive.

Romans 6:11 tells us to "count yourselves dead to sin but alive to God in Christ Jesus." God wants us to come alive. He wants to see us attain the whole measure of the fullness of Christ. And He wants to see our lives gradually become brighter as we become more like Him. If we hold on to our past ways, how can we embrace the future? I found that the only way to truly come alive is to relinquish my own way to God and take hold of the way of Christ.

Looking Further

Part of the lyric from the song "Alive" says this: "I used to think that me, myself and I were all that mattered. But you've shown me all this world can give cannot compare to the joy that comes from giving away."[16]

Living as Christ instructed runs contrary to the way the world tells us to live:

- The world says we attain happiness by seeking to gain everything we can. Jesus says we experience true joy not by gaining something, but by giving it up.
- The world says we should be concerned about how much we receive from others, whether that is monetarily or in terms of physical love, affirmation, or praise. Jesus says that we should be concerned with how much we *give*.
- The world tells us to work hard by making our own way, even stepping on others in the process if that's necessary. Jesus says that we are to surrender our will in deference to others, treating them as more important than ourselves.
- The world says we truly live by following after our own dreams, not letting anything stop us from attaining the material success we seek. Jesus says we truly live by walking in obedience to Him.

Living It Out

Being pure in spirit means swimming upstream against a culture that is concerned with lusting after whatever we can get for ourselves. When you are more concerned with giving sacrificial love than with selfishly taking from others, people will take note of the difference. That's the kind of life that honors Christ and gives hope to those around you. When they see you living that way, they will be motivated to do the same. What decisions will you make today that will testify that you have chosen to live your life not by following the crowd but by following the beat of a different drummer—Jesus? Ask Him to help you fully live life the way He intended.

DAY SEVENTY-FOUR

It Is Well

I can't wait to hear what he'll say. GOD'S about to pronounce his people well, the holy people he loves so much, so they'll never again live like fools. See how close his salvation is to those who fear him? Our country is home base for Glory!

—Psalm 85:8-9, THE MESSAGE

Reflection

Over the centuries, the hymn "It Is Well with My Soul" has offered comfort to thousands of hurting souls. In 1873, Horatio Gates Spafford penned the words in a boat as he was passing over the same ocean waters where his four daughters tragically drowned. I recorded that hymn on September 11, 2001. I was on a plane flying back alone from Florida to a recording session in Nashville at the very hour the planes hit the World Trade Center towers in New York City. I was totally unaware of what had happened that morning until we landed—it immediately became a shocking reality. As we disembarked, we were instantly bombarded with the horrific images of destruction that flashed on television screens all throughout the concourse. People stood in clusters riveted by unbelief—many weeping openly and leaning on each other for comfort.

I vividly remember arriving at the studio. The somber tone was there, as it was everywhere. We gathered in stunned silence to watch what was unfolding. How could we think about being creative amid such anguish? Watching those scenes on TV I thought, *How on earth can I be joyful in my vocals when all this pain is happening?* I chose to sing "It Is Well with My Soul" that day because it seemed so appropriate. When the world was dark and seemingly falling apart all around, I could sing those words with joy because I have God in my life. He is the only true and lasting comfort—the only One who can wipe away our tears, support the weight of such profound earthly pain, and offer hope in the midst of it all. That day—as today—God was and is with us. Only with His Son, Jesus, at the center of our lives can we truly say with confidence, "It is well with my soul."

Looking Further

One of the Hebrew names for God is *Jehovah-shammah*. Because of Judah's disobedience to God, God allowed King Nebuchadnezzar of Babylon to attack Judah and take His people into exile. The faith of the Jews was greatly shaken and they asked, "Where is our God?" The prophet Ezekiel, who had witnessed the destruction of a nation God had built and sustained, was sent to speak God's word to them. At the conclusion of his prophecy he shared a vision in the future when God would again pour out His Spirit on the house of Israel and they would be restored. The city where they would dwell, the new Jerusalem, would be named *Jehovah-shammah*—which means "the LORD is there" (Ezek. 48:35).

Ultimately this prophecy was fulfilled in Jesus. God established a new covenant with His people, and put His laws in their hearts. The One who accomplished this was named Immanuel, which means "God with us" (Matt. 1:22-23). Revelation 21:2-3 fulfills the prophecy concerning the new city. John wrote, "I saw the Holy City, the new Jerusalem, coming down out of heaven from God, prepared as a bride beautifully dressed for her husband. And I heard a loud voice from the throne saying, 'Now the dwelling of God is with men, and he will live with them. They will be his people, and God himself will be with them and be their God.'" There will be no more pain, or death, or tears. All will be well, for the Lord will be there!

Living It Out

Have you ever experienced a tragedy in which you desperately needed God to be there in the midst with you? Do you know someone right now in need of that kind of powerful touch from God? He is *Jehovah-shammah* and is ready to meet you where you are. Call on His name.

Day Seventy-five

A Balancing Act

As pressure and stress bear down on me, I find joy in your commands. Your laws are always right; help me to understand them so I may live.

—Psalm 119:143-144, NLT

Reflection

If your life is anything like mine, you're extremely busy. It often doesn't seem like I have enough hours in the day to accomplish all that I think I need to. A few years ago I had to learn a very difficult lesson about the need for balance in my life. In certain seasons of my ministry, I have overtaxed my body, and have paid the consequences. During one of these times I fell ill with Bell's palsy, a paralysis of a facial nerve, which is usually brought on by stress. I was suffering from physical and emotional exhaustion. I didn't have much left to give and came the closest to the point of burnout that I ever want to get—and I don't ever want to go there again.

Yes, I understand completely

God protected me from going too far in this condition and was simply telling me to slow down. His principle of Sabbath rest is recorded all throughout the Bible. God is concerned that we learn to balance ourselves physically and emotionally. Sometimes it's okay to say no. Learning when to rest and when to work hard takes time—but the earlier you can learn balance, the better off you will be.

I consistently strive for balance in my life as well as my

career . . . finding the balance between grace and discipline, rest and work, giving and receiving. I don't want to err on one side or the other. You can give effectively only if you've been filled up. I am a reasonably consistent person, and yet balance seems elusive at times with my schedule. I'm trying to keep some strong boundaries without being too legalistic about them.

The key to achieving balance is turning all aspects of our lives over to God. We must seek Him daily and submit our plans to Him. He doesn't want us carrying around all the worries and fears that stress us out. He wants to shoulder them. He can bring balance into our lives if we will ask Him. ·

Looking Further

During times of extreme stress and pressure, we can choose to medicate or *meditate*. God's Word is full of promises worth meditating on. They offer peace and hope in times of trouble. Hold on to these during those seasons when you feel out of balance and are in need of God's rest in your spirit:

- "My soul finds rest in God alone; my salvation comes from him" (Ps. 62:1).
- "You will keep in perfect peace all who trust in you, all whose thoughts are fixed on you!" (Isa. 26:3, NLT).
- "Are you tired? Worn out? Burned out on religion? Come to me. Get away with me and you'll recover your life. I'll show you how to take a real rest. Walk with me and work with me—watch how I do it. Learn the unforced rhythms of grace. I won't lay anything heavy or ill-fitting on you. Keep company with me and you'll learn to live freely and lightly" (Matt. 11:28-30, THE MESSAGE).

"We are pressed on every side by troubles, but we are not crushed. We are perplexed, but not driven to despair" (2 Cor. 4:8, NLT).

"Give all your worries and cares to God, for he cares about you" (I Pet. 5:7, NLT).

Living It Out

Plan a day when you can just get away and be with the Lord one-on-one. Do you live near the beach, the mountains, a quiet stream, or some other wonder of God's creation? Go there, take God's Word and a blank journal and a pen—and with no specific agenda (except possibly a nap), be still before the Lord. Allow Him to slow down your racing mind. Give Him your cares and worries; then rest in Him.

DAY SEVENTY-SIX

An Attitude of Gentleness

As God's chosen people, holy and dearly loved, clothe yourselves with compassion, kindness, humility, gentleness and patience.

—Colossians 3:12

Reflection

What does it mean to be a woman of God? I think we need to redefine the traits of real women and focus on a God-honoring femininity. We need to be warm and embracing—which is the opposite of the negative attitude that encourages ill will toward men and a selfish spirit. I want to be a woman who is feminine and who has a soft heart because I trust that God is going to take care of me. I want to have a warmth that draws others and embraces the men God puts in my life, knowing that He has put them there to nurture and protect me—not to stifle my potential.

We need to follow Jesus' example of gentleness and compassion. He drew little children to Himself and made time for them. He reached out to the helpless and the outcast, the lame and the blind. There is a powerful story told in three of the Gospels (Matt. 9; Mark 5; Luke 8). As Jesus was on His way to raise the daughter of Jairus, a synagogue ruler, from the dead, a woman who had been bleeding for twelve years came up behind Jesus and touched the edge of His cloak. The narratives record that she had spent all she had on doctors but to no avail. When she touched the bottom of His garment, the bleeding *immediately* stopped.

Jesus wanted to know who had touched Him, because He actually felt power go out of Him. When the woman came forward and told Jesus she was the one, she trembled before Him and fell at His feet, not knowing what would happen. Jesus said to her, "Daughter, your faith has healed you. Go in peace." How gracious He was in healing her after all her years of suffering. Jesus was gentle and compassionate to all those who were hurting. I continually pray that I will respond the same way to the people in my life.

Looking Further

We don't know the exact nature of her condition, but the woman Jesus healed suffered from some sort of chronic hemorrhaging. According to the regulations laid out in Leviticus 15:25-27 about a "woman who has a discharge of blood," she was considered unclean. Everything and everyone she touched was infected by her uncleanness. The greatest tragedy is that she was cut off from worshipping with others in the temple. No doubt that is why she did not come openly to Jesus, but snuck up through the crowd, hoping to be undetected. She was desperate for a touch from God—and she got it!

Living It Out

Gentleness is one of the nine parts of the fruit of the Spirit (see Gal. 5:22-23) that should characterize a Christian's life. Paul told us in Philippians 4:5 to "let your gentleness be evident to all. The Lord is near." If you knew Jesus was returning to earth tomorrow, would you be a more compassionate person today? Do you know someone who is hurting and desperate for a touch from God? Act as if Jesus is coming back tomorrow, and see what a difference that thought makes in your outlook toward others today.

DAY SEVENTY-SEVEN

A Persevering Spirit

Make every effort to add to your faith goodness; and to goodness, knowledge; and to knowledge, self-control; and to self-control, perseverance; and to perseverance, godliness.

—2 Peter 1:5-6

Reflection

Me too From time to time I get really exhausted out on the road, and start praying, "Oh, God, please give me strength to do this because I can't keep going on my own." I'm constantly around people, so I want to set the right example. I don't want to be down in the dumps, selfish, or grumpy. I want to have a servant attitude. In those times my prayer is, "God, be close to me; give me strength; I want to rely on You. Speak to my heart and fill me so I won't run on empty but will run on overflow."

I've seen the power of God again and again. Sometimes God speaks to my heart about a certain issue only He could know about. He speaks in the quiet of my heart, through the Bible, or through a person—and gives me the answer to exactly what I'm going through. That kind of personal communication with God is available to anyone seeking Him.

It's an old cliché, but it is so true: "When the going gets tough, the tough get going." We may not always understand the things that are happening in our lives or why they are happening. When things occur that make no sense, we have several choices: we can cower in fear and attempt to run away from our difficulties, we can blame God for the circumstances, or we can draw near to Him and ask Him to give us strength and peace. There are times when there *are* no apparent answers—in those times we must simply hang on to God for dear life.

Looking Further

The writers of the New Testament offered encouragement to believers in Jesus during times of intense persecution. After Jesus' resurrection and return to heaven, the believers were persecuted, and many were martyred for their faith in Him. Stephen was the first person mentioned in the Bible to die by stoning as a result of his testimony concerning Jesus. The apostle James was put to death with the sword at the hands of King Herod. Tradition holds that Peter was crucified upside down, his brother Andrew suffered martyrdom in Greece, and Philip was crucified under the Roman emperor Domitian.

The author of Hebrews shared these words concerning many saints who persevered:

> Through acts of faith, they toppled kingdoms, made justice work, took the promises for themselves. They were protected from lions, fires, and sword thrusts, turned disadvantage to advantage, won battles, routed alien armies. Women received their loved ones back from the dead. There were those who, under torture, refused to give in and go free, preferring something better: resurrection. Others braved abuse and whips, and, yes, chains and dungeons. We have stories of those who were stoned, sawed in two, murdered in cold blood; stories of vagrants

wandering the earth in animal skins, homeless, friendless, powerless—the world didn't deserve them!—making their way as best they could on the cruel edges of the world. (Heb. 11:33-38, THE MESSAGE)

Paul encouraged believers to rejoice in their sufferings—knowing that suffering produces perseverance, perseverance yields character, and character brings hope (see Rom. 5:3-4). James pointed out that the testing of our faith brings about perseverance, and perseverance contributes to our spiritual maturity (see James 1:3-4). Peter told his readers not to be surprised by the sufferings they were undergoing, but rather to rejoice and consider themselves blessed to participate in Christ's sufferings (see I Pet. 4:12-19).

Living It Out

Compared to those who were martyred for their faith, your problems may not seem that big after all. But they are there nonetheless, and God cares about them. What are the things that burn you out and make you feel as if you can't go on? Don't try to carry the burdens on your own. You were never meant to. Lay them at Jesus' feet, and trust Him for the outcome. Praise Him for what He will do. Then persevere.

DAY SEVENTY-EIGHT

Waiting for God's Best

I pray to GOD—my life a prayer—and wait for what he'll say and do. My life's on the line before God, my Lord, waiting and watching till morning, waiting and watching till morning.

—Psalm 130:5-6, THE MESSAGE

Reflection

I'm often asked how I remain patient with God's plan for my life when I'm still single. I've talked so much about it, it's no secret—eventually I want to get married. The truth is that there have been many moments when I've been tired of waiting for the right guy to arrive. My mum challenged me once. "You need to let go and trust God with this," she said. I started tearing up. She was right. I asked, "How do you let go of something so important?"

Relinquishing this to God has been quite a process, but I don't want anything for myself that God doesn't want for me. Where are the joy and abundant life in settling for something that He doesn't desire for my life? Releasing this was incredibly freeing. I still believe God will grant me this desire, but I will trust God either way. Until you come to that place of abandonment, the grass always looks greener on the other side. If you can't surrender something of such importance, the danger is that when it comes you will cling to it and suffocate it, and you may end up hurting the very thing you have longed for. I now feel that I will be able to go into marriage as a whole person.

A better prayer than "God, when will You bring the special guy into my life?" is "God, I don't know what You have in mind for my future . . . but I await whatever it is expectantly, knowing that You know me better than I even know myself." I don't want any less than what God has in mind. I want the *best* that He has in mind.

Looking Further

Have you ever waited for something so long that when it actually happened it wasn't nearly as exciting as you hoped it would be? Have you ever longed to open a Christmas gift, and after you did, felt disheartened? Have you ever anticipated an event but when the big day arrived, you were less than overwhelmed? Have you ever had a dream so vivid and incredible that when you woke up you were disappointed to discover it wasn't real life? These experiences can be really frustrating. We certainly don't want our expectations to let us down in marriage, and if we're not careful, we can live in a fantasy world concerning wedded bliss that can never be realized in true life. On the other hand, God's plans for us may be far beyond what we have imagined for ourselves. The prophet Isaiah spoke these words:

> Since the world began, no ear has heard, and no eye has seen a God like you, who works for those who wait for him! You welcome those who gladly do good, who follow godly ways. (Isa. 64:4-5, NLT)

The key while we wait on Him, Isaiah says, is to continue to walk with God, getting on with life and doing good.

Living It Out

Have you placed your life and your future completely in God's hands? If not, as you have your palms open and facing the ground, tell God that you want to relinquish your personal desires. Then turn your opened palms over so that they face heaven, and tell your Father that you surrender your future to His will for your life. It's a scary prayer, but one that God will certainly honor.

DAY SEVENTY-NINE

When Waiting Gets Tough

God, the one and only—I'll wait as long as he says. Everything I need comes from him, so why not? He's solid rock under my feet, breathing room for my soul, an impregnable castle: I'm set for life.

—Psalm 62:1-2, THE MESSAGE

Reflection

When I'm experiencing a dry spell on this waiting-for-marriage front, sometimes a romantic novel or movie helps keep that spark of hope going. During tough seasons, as a hopeful (not hopeless) romantic, it helps me to recall how God has been constant and faithful to me in times past. God is God, no matter what.

A few years ago I found myself hanging on to my longing for love and a husband, that deep desire of my life. I felt that I needed to control it, that I couldn't trust God with it and couldn't really let it go to Him. That's when He called me to lay my dream of marriage down, to take my hands off. I think many single women are afraid to do this. Too often we think, *If I give this up to God, He's going to require lifelong singleness. I need to know what God is going to do before I will give up this dream.* When we hold on, trying to protect ourselves and thinking we're making our lives much better by handling it on our own, we're actually forgetting God's character.

When I affirmed my prayerful words to God, "I'll love You even if You don't provide a husband for me, and I'll trust that You know what's best for me." I found such amazing peace. My goal is to stay surrendered to Him regardless of the immediate circumstances. I know that God wants what's best for me and that He is going to take care of me. He has proved Himself faithful to me so many times before, and I have no reason to doubt because I know that His perfect plan is always the best.

Looking Further

The apostle Paul faced many difficult trials. Through them he learned how to wait on God's faithfulness in the midst of the tough times he had to endure. He prayed this prayer for the Colossian believers:

> Be assured that from the first day we heard of you, we haven't stopped praying for you, asking God to give you wise minds and spirits attuned to his will, and so acquire a thorough understanding of the ways in which God works. We pray that you'll live well for the Master, making him proud of you as you work hard in his orchard. As you learn more and more how God works, you will learn how to do your work. We pray that you'll have the strength to

*merely
— surviving
vs. joy*

stick it out over the long haul—not the grim strength of gritting your teeth but the glory-strength God gives. It is strength that endures the unendurable and spills over into joy, thanking the Father who makes us strong enough to take part in everything bright and beautiful that he has for us. (Col. 1:9-12, THE MESSAGE)

And to the believers in Rome, Paul shared these powerful words:

Hope that is seen is no hope at all. Who hopes for what he already has? But if we hope for what we do not yet have, we wait for it patiently. (ROMANS 8:24-25)

Living It Out

Ask God today to reveal more of His will and wisdom in your life. Then ask Him for a greater ability to understand His purposes in your life. Ask Him for patience and confidence in His plan as you wait for Him. Thank Him for what He will accomplish as He uses you for His glory.

DAY EIGHTY

Real Success

I'm asking GOD for one thing, only one thing: to live with him in his house my whole life long. I'll contemplate his beauty; I'll study at his feet. That's the only quiet, secure place in a noisy world, the perfect getaway, far from the buzz of traffic.

—Psalm 27:4-5, THE MESSAGE

Reflection

Are you a list girl? I love my lists. There's nothing like the feeling of accomplishment when I have a to-do list with all its boxes checked because all the items have been completed! So many of us women are wired to be doers, aren't we? When you think about it, our obsession with marking things off a to-do list can often be a worldly success thing. We feel successful and efficient when we cross something off our lists. But I've felt God tell me, "Spend time with Me even if it doesn't seem 'efficient.' Just love Me and allow Me to love you."

Whenever I pull away from the day-to-day to have an extended time with God, He teaches me the importance of *being*, not just *doing*. I like to go for walks with God, where I can listen to nature or stare into the sky. I love being outside in God's creation, delighting in this world He's given us. At times He wants us to just *be* with Him, and not accomplish anything. Sometimes I sit and read a book in a hammock at my parents' place. Even if you don't have much downtime, you can take mini-sabbaticals, like taking a couple of hours between tasks.

I saw a sign in front of a local church that said this: "The world honors success. God honors faithfulness." "Just learn to rest in Me," God says. "I'm not requiring anything of you." Isaiah 30:15 says, "In repentance and rest is your salvation, in quietness and trust is your strength." It's about Him; it's not about us. Knowing that should really free us to focus on trying to be faithful to His plan for our lives. And at the end of the day, that's real success.

Looking Further

I love the story of Mary of Bethany in the New Testament. Jesus and His disciples were on their way to her home in search of an oasis of calm in the midst of some pretty intense weeks leading up to the Cross. Her older sister, Martha, was appropriately named. Martha Stewart had nothing on her! Luke 10:40 says that she "was distracted by all the preparations that had to be made." She was stressed. Everything had to be just so. She was so bothered that she asked Jesus to intervene. She approached Him and asked if He cared that she was doing all the work while Mary did nothing but sit at Jesus' feet "listening to what he said" (v. 39). Mary was soaking in every shred of truth spoken by the Master, and she hung on His every word.

Jesus responded to Martha, "My dear Martha, you are worried and upset over all these details! There is only one thing worth being concerned about. Mary has discovered it, and it will not be taken away from her" (Luke 10:41-42, NLT). Martha thought that many things were necessary for the Lord's comfort, and she was wearing herself out in an effort to provide them. But Jesus was more concerned about just *being* with them and sharing life, and Mary's devotion was more important than any of the delicious food Martha had prepared. How easy it is to get distracted with so many things competing for our attention, when only one thing is really needed—intimacy with Jesus.

Living It Out

Do you tend to be more like Martha or more like Mary? What distracts you from seeking intimacy with Jesus? What can you do today to just *be* with Him?

DAY EIGHTY-ONE

Pursuing the Arts

Make a careful exploration of who you are and the work you have been given, and then sink yourself into that. Don't be impressed with yourself. Don't compare yourself with others. Each of you must take responsibility for doing the creative best you can with your own life.

—Galatians 6:4-5, THE MESSAGE

Francis Schaeffer, founder of the L'Abri Fellowship Study Center in Huemoz, Switzerland, where I visited a couple of years ago, said this: "Art is a reflection of God's creativity, an evidence that we are made in the image of God."[17] God's very nature is to create, and He loves it when His children embrace their God-given creativity. One of the artistic outlets I greatly enjoy in my ministry is the making of music videos, giving me the opportunity to really think outside the box. My most enjoyable experience to date was probably shooting the video for the song "Reborn." I got to be part of a very unique and artistic setting for this video shoot. I had the chance to dress up in a funky orange skirt, hand a large ostrich-size egg to a child in an acting part of the video, and watch an Asian martial arts performer do what he does best!

There are some exciting things going on right now as followers of Christ get more involved in the arts. For instance, more doors seem to be open in our culture for family films and faith-based films these days. For so long it seemed as though true artists couldn't find their place in the church. But now many churches have started ministries that encourage the members of the body to use their artistic gifts for God's glory—in media such as drawing, painting, dance, pottery, theater, scriptwriting, set design, and video production. There are so many cool ways in which we can uniquely impact people's senses with God's message today. It's time for God's people to seize the day in the arena of the arts.

We can't just settle for the status quo in our spiritual growth or in the way we choose to express it. Our culture is moving incredibly fast. We have to move with the times, staying on our toes so we don't become irrelevant. You can opt to just coast along, doing the same old, same old. It's safer, less risky, but where's the adventure? Where's the exhilaration? Where's the "seize the day" mentality in that? I don't know about you, but I'm not a coasting kind of girl. God has created us to enjoy life to its fullest, and He delights Himself in our creative pursuits.

Looking Further

When Moses was instructed by God to design the ark of the covenant, the tabernacle, and all the various altars, tables, and utensils, God provided him the skill he needed. God Himself specifically chose an artist named Bezalel, from the tribe of Judah, to spearhead the creative work. About him God said, "I have filled him with the Spirit of God, giving him great wisdom, ability, and expertise in all kinds of crafts. He is a master craftsman, expert in working with gold, silver, and bronze. He is skilled in engraving and mounting gemstones and in carving wood. He is a master at every craft!" (Exod. 31:3-5, NLT). Can you imagine how this artist must have been empowered, knowing he was specifically chosen by the Creator of the universe to carry out God's specs for the design of His tabernacle and all its furnishings, as well as the sacred vestments of the priests?

When God asked Solomon to build a temple in His name in Jerusalem, Solomon knew he would need skilled artists and craftsmen. He put out a plea to Hiram, king of Tyre. The king replied, "I am sending you a master craftsman named Huramabi, who is extremely talented. . . . He is skillful at making things from gold, silver, bronze, and iron, and he also works with stone and wood. He can work with purple, blue, and scarlet cloth and fine linen. He is also an engraver and can follow any design given to him. He will work with your craftsmen and those appointed by my lord David, your father" (2 Chron. 2:13-14, NLT). God is serious about beautiful design adorning where He chooses to dwell. And, just as He uniquely gifted these artisans for the intricate work of designing His temple, He has blessed you with specific talents for use in glorifying His name.

Living It Out

What talents have you been blessed with? How are you using them to glorify God? He delights in whatever you bring to the table. The more you use your gifts to glorify Him, the more He will develop them.

DAY EIGHTY-TWO

Spirit Touching Spirit

It's who you are and the way you live that count before God. Your worship must engage your spirit in the pursuit of truth. That's the kind of people the Father is out looking for: those who are simply and honestly themselves before him in their worship. God is sheer being itself—Spirit. Those who worship him must do it out of their very being, their spirits, their true selves, in adoration.

—John 4:23-24, THE MESSAGE

Reflection

When I was growing up, I often stayed at my grandparents' home. They owned a beautiful, multistoried house, with flower gardens and fruit trees. One of the sweetest things was waking up in the morning to the familiar sound of birds singing outside my window. For the most part they were rainbow lorikeets, whose song is more like a screech than anything else, but to my ears it was beautiful. To God's ears, the birds' singing was also beautiful because it represented their song of love to Him—a song of gratefulness for life and a new day. That experience inspired me to write "Song of Love." It doesn't matter to God how well we can sing. What matters is the pure worship He receives, that our hearts are singing our own unique songs of worship. The love of God is what draws us, keeps us, and invites us to worship Him.

Writing worship songs to God is one of my favorite things about being in ministry. It's awesome to record albums composed entirely of worship songs. And it's a beautiful thing to have the experience of God birthing a song in my heart and then letting me hear an audience use that song to worship God too!

One of my all-time favorite worship songs is "Quiet You with My Love," which comes out of Zephaniah 3:17. It's really God's love song to us. I picture God as our "Daddy" saying, "Hush, My child, be still. Rest in My arms. Let Me hold you." We are created to worship God, to adore Him, and to be in fellowship with Him. The joy that comes from that is a beautiful gift. Worship consists of our prayers of the heart, prayers of love, saying, "God, thank You for who You are." We adore and marvel at God's amazing power and love for us.

I have been a member of the same church in my hometown for a number of years, but recently my worship pastor moved and I was able to help out by leading worship. I used to come home from being on the road and just want to soak it in, just wanted to be fed because I was exhausted and had nothing left. But I have loved getting to contribute as a worship leader because the focus isn't on me, and I get to help others celebrate our wonderful Savior.

Looking Further

The dramatic encounter in John 4 between Jesus and the Samaritan woman at the well of Sychar provides a wonderful glimpse into the kind of worship that pleases our Father. First of all, the fact that Jesus engaged a woman in conversation is a testimony to the value God places on every human being. In those days, strict rabbis forbade teachers to greet women in public—and especially if those women were Samaritans! After Jesus revealed that He knew the woman's promiscuous life story without her providing any details, she knew that He was a "prophet," so she queried Him on the correct location to worship—where the Samaritans worshipped or where the Jews worshipped at the temple in Jerusalem. Jesus pointed out that true worship has nothing to do with location, but everything to do with attitude. He said that God was seeking people who desired to worship Him in spirit and truth.

True worship is when we, through our spirits (made in the image of God), draw close in friendship and intimacy with our Maker. Genuine worship is when we sincerely seek all of God's truth and when our spirits crave meeting with God. The woman responded that she knew she would understand more when the Messiah came. Can't you just see her jaw dropping to the ground as Jesus delivered His parting words, "I who speak to you am he" (John 4:26)? The woman was so excited that she ran to tell others about Him and left her water jar there at the well. Many of the people from her village believed in Jesus because of the woman's testimony, "He told me everything I ever did" (v. 29). True worship and adoration draws others to Jesus.

Living It Out

Are you the kind of worshipper the Father is seeking? Do you crave times of being alone with Him? Set aside some time today to do just that.

DAY EIGHTY-THREE

God's Plans vs. Ours

You can make many plans, but the LORD's purpose will prevail.

—Proverbs 19:21, NLT

Reflection

I recently had a great experience that reminded me God's plans are always superior to my own. I had a very unique and interesting show in Pigeon Forge, Tennessee, but it almost got rained out. Since they had an indoor café section at the venue, we were able to reassemble everyone out of the rain. We did a rather impromptu, very postponed acoustic show for those who stayed to brave the elements. The night ended up being a very moving time of community, family, and real connection. Something that could've been very disappointing for many people actually turned out to be a more powerful worship experience than we would have had originally in the large, but not intimate, amphitheater. Praise God that He turned that around!

Even when we can't see the sun because it is obscured behind the rain and clouds, God is always working out everything for the good of those who love Him and are called according to His purpose (see Rom. 8:28). One of my favorite books in the Bible is the letter written by James. The Holy Spirit speaks through him on many different issues in a very straightforward, gripping, in-your-face kind of way. Regarding our plans vs. God's, James says this:

I have a word for you who brashly announce, "Today—at the latest, tomorrow—we're off to such and such a city for the year. We're going to start a business and make a lot of money." You don't know the first thing about tomorrow. You're nothing but a wisp of fog, catching a brief bit of sun before disappearing. Instead, make it a habit to say, "If the Master wills it and we're still alive, we'll do this or that." As it is, you are full of your grandiose selves. All such vaunting self-importance is evil. (4:13-16, THE MESSAGE)

We should live our lives with an attitude of "planned spontaneity" because we do not know what tomorrow will bring. It's certainly not wrong to plan trips, schedule appointments, be involved in community and church events, and keep regular dates on our calendar. But we must realize that all of our plans should always be subject to God's intervention if He has something else in mind for us to accomplish. Often what we may perceive as obstacles or interruptions, God may be providing as opportunities for personal growth and ministry to others.

Looking Further

Here are some other truths regarding the Lord's plans for our lives:

- ✓ "The LORD's plans stand firm forever; his intentions can never be shaken" (Ps. 33:11, NLT).
- ✓ "In his heart a man plans his course, but the LORD determines his steps" (Prov. 16:9).
- ✓ "The LORD directs our steps, so why try to understand everything about the way?" (Prov. 20:24, NLT).

✓ "The LORD Almighty has sworn, 'Surely, as I have planned, so it will be, and as I have purposed, so it will stand'" (Isa. 14:24).

✓ "I know, LORD, that our lives are not our own. We are not able to plan our own course" (Jer. 10:23, NLT).

Living It Out

Has God ever intervened in your life and brought about something way better than you originally had planned? Have you ever been guilty of making a decision and forging ahead of His will, then suffering the consequences? Are there some immediate plans you have made that you need to submit to the Lord? Choose several of the Scriptures listed above and read them aloud to God in your quiet time with Him. Then strive to live today according to those truths.

DAY EIGHTY-FOUR

Strangely Warmed

We saw it, we heard it, and now we're telling you so you can experience it along with us, this experience of communion with the Father and his Son, Jesus Christ. . . . If we walk in the light, God himself being the light, we also experience a shared life with one another, as the sacrificed blood of Jesus, God's Son, purges all our sin.

—1 John 1:3, 7, THE MESSAGE

Reflection

This past summer I traveled to the Czech Republic for the first time. Concerts like mine are seldom staged in that country. I visited the former Communist nation on the day of their National Youth Gathering in the city of Tabor. I had an audience of more than seven thousand Czech young people who jumped, clapped, and sang their way through the entire concert—it was like a massive sea of people in motion. During the song "Forgive Me," almost everyone raised their hands in surrender to God. From what the organizers said, I'm sure for many in the crowd this was their first experience with Christianity.

Europe is almost like a second home to me. I always love going there because there's such a fresh enthusiasm for the musical, spiritual encouragement we bring. I've visited a number of countries several times and have built up a kind of supportive family—seeing them is like coming back to visit relatives. I feel a real sense of community with them, and through them my heart has been "strangely warmed" by Jesus' love. When I return back home I'm refreshed, much as the two men were who walked with Jesus on the way to Emmaus.

We take Communion to remember the central truth of our faith—that Jesus died for our sins, rose again from the grave, and is alive. He asked us to partake of the bread and the wine with our brothers and sisters in Christ regularly so that we wouldn't forget His incredible sacrifice. Part of the lyric to the song, "Lest I Forget," says,

Lord, you wept tears of blood for me,
You hung in agony so deep,
Carried my sin away for good.
Now, I, I take this bread and wine
Remembering your love divine.
You walked through fire to free my soul.[18]

Whether we're communing with the saints on another continent or sharing the Lord's Supper in our local church, something powerful happens when we gather with the body of Christ and partake of His goodness.

Looking Further

After Jesus' resurrection from the tomb, Luke 24 recounts the story of two disciples who were headed to a village called Emmaus, which was seven miles west of Jerusalem. One of them was named Cleopas. They were discussing all the events that had taken place surrounding Jesus' death, burial, and resurrection. Jesus came up and walked beside them, but they were "kept from recognizing him" (v. 16). They dialogued with Jesus about recent events; then He explained a number of things about the Messiah, beginning with Moses and the prophets—and they still didn't know who He was.

Jesus ended up staying with the two men and eating dinner with them. "When he was at the table with them, he took bread, gave thanks, broke it and began to give it to them. Then their eyes were opened and they recognized him, and he disappeared from their sight. They asked each other, 'Were not our hearts burning within us while he talked with us on the road and opened the Scriptures to us?'" (Luke 24:30-32).

It's interesting that they did not recognize Jesus until He broke the bread and gave it to them. Perhaps they had seen those same hands break the loaves and feed the five thousand (see Matt. 14:13–21). As they ate and fellowshipped with Him, suddenly the blinders were removed from their eyes, and they knew His true identity. Powerful things happen when we gather in community with Jesus Christ and fellow believers. We stand strong together!

Living It Out

Spend a few moments thinking about some of the best times you've had sharing life with other members of the body of Christ. How have you been refreshed by spending time with them? Give thanks to God for that kind of fellowship, which is possible because of what Jesus accomplished for you on the cross. Then drop a card in the mail thanking someone for sharing authentically with you.

DAY EIGHTY-FIVE

Living Authentically

May integrity and honesty protect me, for I put my hope in you.

—Psalm 25:21, NLT

Reflection

Australians are known for their direct, straightforward, in-your-face approach when it comes to speaking to others. I was fourteen years old when my family moved to America and dived straight into the heart of American culture, in an area of the country widely known for its southern hospitality—Nashville, Tennessee. I found this to be a lovely thing for the most part. But I had a hard time adjusting when I heard "Let's get together" and "Let's do lunch" from people who didn't really mean what they said.

How do you know whether someone really means what she is saying? How do you know when she is really being authentic? How can you tell when someone is not sincere, but just trying to be nice? A girl befriended me in church while I was still very new to America. She was very pleasant and warm to me. Then after two months she abruptly backed off and wasn't as nice anymore. I discovered later that she had been asked by a Sunday school teacher to befriend me because I was the new kid. I remember being very hurt by that. I would've preferred not to have that friendship at all, because it wasn't real.

In Jesus' parable of the soils, He spoke about the seed that fell into the fertile soil and grew up to produce a large crop. Luke 8:15 says, "The seeds that fell on the good soil represent honest, good-hearted people who hear God's word, cling to it, and patiently produce a huge harvest" (NLT). God places great importance on our being honest in our hearts and walking in truth with one another. By living out that truth, we will bear much fruit. Jesus died so that we could lead a life of freedom in Him—free from our sins, and free from the lies so prevalent in the world around us. One of the ways we can live out the full expression of the freedom He has given us is by being authentic with one another.

Looking Further

After Philip first met Jesus, he told his friend Nathanael that he had seen the Messiah they had been waiting for, and because Nazareth was not known to be a place of nobility, Nathanael questioned, "Can anything good come from there?" (John 1:46). When Jesus saw Nathanael approaching Him, He could see straight into his heart and He affirmed his authenticity: "Now here is a genuine son of Israel—a man of complete integrity" (v. 47, NLT). *The Message* translates that verse, "There's a real Israelite, not a false bone in his body." We don't know much else about Nathanael from the Bible record, but he certainly could not have received any greater commendation than what Jesus said about him.

King David said, "What joy for those whose record the LORD has cleared of guilt, whose lives are lived in complete honesty!" (Ps. 32:2, NLT). When there's nothing to hide, there's nothing to be ashamed of. David also proclaimed,

Does anyone want to live a life that is long and prosperous? Then keep your tongue from speaking evil and your lips from telling lies! Turn away from evil and do good. Search for peace, and work to maintain it. (Ps. 34:12-14, NLT)

Living It Out

As you live with others, is it easy or hard for you to be completely honest? What keeps you from being authentic with those closest to you? Give your fears about that over to God; then take the risk to be vulnerable, and watch what happens.

Day Eighty-six

No Secrets

Honesty lives confident and carefree, but Shifty is sure to be exposed. An evasive eye is a sign of trouble ahead, but an open, face-to-face meeting results in peace.

—Proverbs 10:9-10, The Message

Reflection

During my teenage years, my parents instituted a "no secrets" policy in our family. They encouraged my siblings and me to share what was going on in our lives—both the good and the bad. They, in turn, were open with us about their own struggles, so they visibly modeled that openness for us. Because of that modeling, I was able to be really open and honest with my parents and treat them like friends. It was a wonderful support system, and I reaped the benefits of their spiritual encouragement, practical wisdom, and advice.

The no-secrets policy helped me get through a difficult time that I experienced in my early twenties. I had moved away from home and was really struggling with loneliness, exhaustion, and emotional upheaval after a challenging thirteen-month road tour and a mission trip to Romania. I struggled with sadness, wondering if there was a light at the end of the tunnel. During that time people often asked me, "How are you doing?" And I usually replied, "Well, actually not so good. It's kind of a hard season right now," rather than just saying, "Fine."

My honesty with people was a catalyst for inviting prayers from others who helped me survive that dark period. Being vulnerable and authentic is a very important part of our fellowship as Christians. If we constantly put up walls and say, "I'm okay!" we communicate, "I'm perfect; I have everything together; I don't need anyone." That pushes people away, and in the process they are often left to feel that they have problems no one else understands. When we open up and take the risk of being real, we realize that those around us have many of the same issues, hurts, and problems we have. It is only in an atmosphere of honesty that we are able to authentically minister to one another.

There is definitely an appropriate time and place for sharing intimate details of our lives with others. I've walked onstage on days when the going was tough. But that's not the time for me to unload on my audience about what I'm struggling with. There has to be sensitivity to others. We can't always expose exactly what we are feeling at the expense of others. But by having a no-secrets policy with close friends and family, we are faithfully led to the ultimate truth: Where there are no secrets, there are no lies.

Looking Further

Jesus calls us to live our lives in such a way that we have nothing to hide. He doesn't want us to live one way onstage before others and another way behind the scenes. If we are walking in God's truth, striving to please Him, we will have no problem living a no-secrets life. Jesus challenges us in Mark 4:21-22:

> Does anyone bring a lamp home and put it under a washtub or beneath the bed? Don't you put it up on a table or on the mantel? We're not keeping secrets, we're telling them; we're not hiding things, we're bringing them out into the open. (THE MESSAGE)

Living It Out

Have you ever been tempted to play the role of a secret agent, living two distinct lives? If you've ever acted that out, how did you feel? Talk to God about your desire to live in complete honesty with Him and with those He has surrounded you with for community and support. Thank Him for His provision.

DAY EIGHTY-SEVEN

In Need of Hope

The LORD helps the fallen and lifts those bent beneath their loads. The eyes of all look to you in hope; you give them their food as they need it. When you open your hand, you satisfy the hunger and thirst of every living thing.

—Psalm 145:14-16, NLT

Reflection

I vividly remember the time I spent in Romania some years ago. I had really felt called to serve there on a short-term mission trip, working behind the scenes in whatever ways God led me. As I saw how so many homeless people—little children, teens, adults, and entire families—lived right on the streets and in the sewers in the midst of the garbage, I realized that they weren't living full lives. They were living half a life. They were alive . . . but they were dead. Some of them inhaled glue in an attempt to escape the hurt. As I looked into their eyes, they were just *gone*. It wasn't merely because of the drugs or the conditions of their existence. It was the fact that they needed Jesus. A transformation was necessary in their lives if they were to find hope.

In his book *The Irresistible Revolution*, Shane Claiborne challenges the followers of Jesus to abandon the American dream and to rethink what true biblical Christianity should look like in today's culture, especially as it relates to how Christians should be reaching the poor and hurting in real, tangible ways.[19] It might be in the inner city or in the poorest parts of the world. We have an obligation to bring hope to others. But you know what? People in North America and in other rich parts of the world are also in desperate need of hope. They might have a lot more—a nice house, a great car, money—but many people are not really living; they're dead. Everyone everywhere is looking for hope. Everyone everywhere needs Jesus.

Looking Further

Jesus passed through a town called Nain, which was located a few miles southeast of His childhood home of Nazareth. As He and His disciples approached the town gate, they met a funeral procession. The only son of a widow was being carried out for burial. When Jesus saw her, His heart broke for her and He said, "Don't cry." He reached out and touched the coffin, then directed the deceased to get up. When the young man sat up and started talking with his mother, the whole crowd was filled with awe. Luke 7:16-17 records their response:

> They all realized they were in a place of holy mystery, that God was at work among them. They were quietly worshipful—and then noisily grateful, calling out among themselves, "God is back, looking to the needs of his people!" The news of Jesus spread all through the country. (THE MESSAGE)

This is the first of three instances of Jesus' raising someone from the dead, the others being Jairus's daughter (see Luke 8:40-56) and Lazarus (see John 11:38-44). The NIV translates the phrase in Luke 7:16, "God has come to help his people."

On each of these occasions Jesus had tremendous compassion for the grieving and brought them hope. He did the same thing for many others who were physically alive but spiritually dead, and today He still longs to meet *our* need for hope.

Living It Out

Do you feel spiritually alive or dead today? Is there an area of your life that needs to be resurrected by Jesus? He already knows your specific needs, and He wants to provide the hope you long for. Confess your desperate need for Him, and then give Him free rein to accomplish His will in your life.

DAY EIGHTY-EIGHT

Real Love

We know what real love is because Jesus gave up his life for us. So we also ought to give up our lives for our brothers and sisters. If someone has enough money to live well and sees a brother or sister in need but shows no compassion—how can God's love be in that person? Dear children, let's not merely say that we love each other; let us show the truth by our actions.

—1 John 3:16-18, NLT

Reflection

While vacationing in Australia one year, thoughts of the last chapter of John jumped out at me in a powerful way. A passage describes something that took place a few weeks after Jesus had risen from the dead. Jesus was sitting around a campfire, eating breakfast with Peter and some of the other disciples. After breakfast, Jesus turned to Peter and asked, "Peter, do you love Me?"

Peter answered, "Yes, Lord, You know that I love You."

Jesus said, "Feed My sheep."

Then He again asked Peter, "Do you love Me?"

And once again, Peter responded, "Yes, Lord, You know that I do."

"Then feed My lambs."

And one more time Jesus asked, "Peter do you *really* love Me?" By now, Peter must have been freaking out, thinking, *Why would He ask me a third time? What have I done?*

"Yes, Lord, You *know* that I love You with all my heart."

And Jesus again said, "Feed My sheep."

There is something incredibly powerful about Jesus' repeating His question to Peter (and to us) three times. Remember when you were a child and your mom told you to do something? The first time she said it, you kind of half listened. She repeated it a second time, and you took a bit more notice. But the third time, she used your full name—first, middle, and last—and you knew she meant business! That's the effect Jesus had when He asked Peter the same question again and again. And as I read that passage, I felt God's challenge to me too. I sensed God asking me, "Rebecca, do you love Me? Then feed My lambs."

I began to ask myself: *Who are the people God is calling me to feed? Are they my family, my friends, or people who don't yet know Jesus? Am I being faithful to feed the "sheep" Jesus has placed in my life? If not, how can I change that?* I really believe that Jesus is calling all of us to take action and respond to His penetrating question. Do you love Him? Then feed the sheep in your life. It's a daily responsibility and an urgent need.

Looking Further

Others will not necessarily know that we are followers of Christ if all we do is believe the right things. They won't know that we are sold out to Jesus if we have the books of the Bible memorized, or if we have perfect attendance at church. They won't be impacted by what we *say* we believe. Jesus said, "Your love for one another will prove to the world that you are my disciples" (John 13:35, NLT). That is the thing that will set us apart from the way much of the rest of the world lives. We are called to an unselfish love that sees others' needs and meets them in Jesus' name. First Peter 1:22 says, "You were cleansed from your sins when you obeyed the truth, so now you must show sincere love to each other as brothers and sisters. Love each other deeply with all your heart" (NLT).

Living It Out

Do you love Him? Do you *love* Him? Do you *really* love Him? Then take a look at the clerk in the grocery store, the person who lives down the street and seems to talk to no one, an unsaved friend, or someone in your family. Love them, care for them, pray for them, pray *with* them, and point them to Jesus. That's real love.

Day Eighty-nine

Hearts Wide Open

Pray for us, for our conscience is clear and we want to live honorably in everything we do.

—Hebrews 13:18, NLT

Reflection

Not too long ago I was greatly impacted by something Ken, my life coach, did. I was sharing about the challenges of keeping balance in ministry. As usual, he listened intently and then brought wisdom to the table. He shared that in his own life he too had struggled with exactly the same thing. I was impressed that he, in his position of leadership, was so vulnerable with me.

Often I've felt that professionalism requires a strong front rather than what many people perceive as weakness. Over the last few years I have learned that sometimes one of the most powerful and surprisingly strong things we can do as leaders is to share vulnerably at appropriate times. This invites beautiful community. We all hurt, and by sharing in this way, led by God, we invite others to relate deeply with us.

I have a very open and honest relationship with my best friend, Karleen. She is married and has four kids. It's amazing that even though she lives in a completely different world from my life, we have so much in common! When we get together we relate on so many levels. Spiritually, she's strong—she brings accountability and encouragement to me. Sometimes we are going through the same things, or have similar challenges in our lives, but they are due to completely different circumstances. I constantly see how God has ordained our friendship and provided us for each other. I see God's beautiful hand on our friendship.

The apostle Paul once wrote these challenging words: "Oh, dear Corinthian friends! We have spoken honestly with you, and our hearts are open to you. There is no lack of love on our part, but you have withheld your love from us. I am asking you to respond as if you were my own children. Open your hearts to us!" (2 Cor. 6:11-13, NLT).

Hearts wide open before others. That's a very cool thought. If we live with purity of spirit, we'll have nothing to hide. We'll have nothing to be ashamed of, no fear of being found out. What a liberating feeling! That doesn't mean we're perfect, just that we are committed to living openly and honestly before others. The Dutch priest Henri Nouwen said that we could be "wounded healers." We may have struggled with certain things in the past, but now we are not looking back; we are looking toward the future. We need to be as vulnerable and open with others as possible as we do life together.

Looking Further

The book of Proverbs offers great wisdom on this theme of the value of living honestly before others:

- "Honesty guides good people; dishonesty destroys treacherous people" (11:3, NLT).
- "The godly are directed by honesty; the wicked fall beneath their load of sin" (11:5, NLT).

"Good leaders cultivate honest speech; they love advisors who tell them the truth" (16:13, THE MESSAGE).

Living It Out

Is there an aspect of living vulnerably before others that is scary? Absolutely. But we were made for community. Sometimes it can be messy, but where would we be without the help of others speaking into our lives? Choose one of the verses above and commit it to memory. Then walk in the truth.

DAY NINETY

A Worship Revolution

GOD made the heavens—royal splendor radiates from him, a powerful beauty sets him apart. Bravo, GOD, Bravo! Everyone join in the great shout: Encore! In awe before the beauty, in awe before the might. Bring gifts and celebrate, bow before the beauty of GOD, then to your knees—everyone worship!

—Psalm 96:5-9, THE MESSAGE

Reflection

God uses nature to call me to worship Him. I am often blown away by the creativity and intricacy—as well as the power—expressed in His creation. I think of a thunderstorm and how so often I've seen the power of God in that. While in Florida not too long ago, I found a very unique coral-shaped sponge on the beach. That discovery was a unique exhibition of God's beauty and creativity to me.

As I have traveled all over the world, from America to Australia to Bulgaria to Holland to Kyrgyzstan, I have witnessed God's power expressed in incredible ways through the people He's created. I've been surprised at how similarly we all are connected with God through worship. You might think that the worship in various cultures would be drastically different, but I've realized that ultimately we are just one family in God. The passion and the heartbeat we feel are the same. That's very encouraging to me.

In the past fifteen years of being in Christian music, I've seen a growing hunger for worship among young people—especially college students. Movements of God like Hillsong United and Passion One Day have really ignited passionate worshippers of God. They desire to be singularly focused on Jesus in their heartfelt and intense times of worship. They're not preoccupied with what others think about their particular expressions of worship. They're more concerned with pleasing God by encountering Him personally.

While in the studio recording the *Worship God* album, I was reading the book of Revelation, and was hit by the idea that one day every knee will bow and every tongue will confess that Jesus Christ is Lord, and we'll all cry out, "Holy is the Lamb." The song "Lamb of God" is a celebration in preparation for that day. As my eyes fell on Revelation 19:6-7, which begins, "I heard what sounded like a great multitude," words and music started to come together in my head. I'm so looking forward to continuing to worship for all eternity with brothers and sisters from all nations and languages and people groups.

Looking Further

The book of Revelation includes descriptions of some powerful worship experiences that will take place in God's ultimate dwelling place, heaven. What we are doing now on earth is a dress rehearsal for what is to come! In John's vision he saw these incredible scenes:

- "I looked and heard the voice of many angels, numbering thousands upon thousands, and ten thousand times ten thousand. They encircled the throne and the living creatures and the elders. In a loud voice they sang: 'Worthy is the Lamb, who was slain, to receive power and wealth and wisdom and strength and honor and glory and praise!' Then I heard every creature in heaven and on earth and under the earth and on the sea, and all that is in them, singing: 'To him who sits on the throne and to the Lamb be praise and honor and glory and power, for ever and ever!'" (Rev. 5:11-13).
- "I heard what sounded like a great multitude, like the roar of rushing waters and like loud peals of thunder, shouting: 'Hallelujah! For our Lord God Almighty reigns. Let us rejoice and be glad and give him glory! For the wedding of the Lamb has come, and his bride has made herself ready'" (Rev. 19:6-7).

Living It Out

When you think about the incredible worship we'll experience in heaven, how does that move you to worship the Lamb of God now? Where is your favorite place to worship God? As part of the bride of Christ, what do you need to do to ready yourself for His return?

Notes

1. *Merriam-Webster's Collegiate Dictionary*, 10th ed., s.v. "pure."

2. Dictionaryreference Web site, http://dictionary.reference.com/browse/hypocrite.

3. Information in this paragraph gleaned from T. D. Manning, "Biblical Worship," *Harbinger, Too* (Orange Park, FL: Orange Park Christian Church, 1983), 100, 116–18.

4. *Merriam-Webster's Collegiate Dictionary*, 10th ed., s.v. "pure."

5. Larry Crabb, *The Pressure's Off: There's a New Way to Live* (Colorado Springs: WaterBrook, 2004).

6. James Strong, *A Concise Dictionary of the Words in the Hebrew Bible* (Nashville, TN: Abingdon Press, 1975), 32, 47, 52, 106.

7. Rebecca St. James, Tedd Tjornhom, Toby McKeehan © 2005 Up in the Mix Music/Rambuka Music (BMI)/Meaux Hits/Tedasia Music (ASCAP)/Achtober Songs (BMI), admin by EMI CMG Publishing.

8. Rebecca St. James, Matt Bronleewe, Jason Ingram © 2005 Up in the Mix Music/Rambuka Music (BMI), admin by EMI CMG Publishing/Aetataureate Music (BMI)/Dayspring Music Publishing (BMI).

9. Rebecca St. James and Lynda Hunter Bjorklund, *SHE: Safe, Healthy, Empowered—The Woman You're Made to Be* (Wheaton, IL: Tyndale, 2004).

10. Scott Dyer, Rebecca St. James © 2005 Ever Devoted Music/ Scott Dyer Publishing Designee (ASCAP)/Up in the Mix Music/ Rambuka Music (BMI), admin by EMI CMG Publishing.

11. Information taken from Rebecca St. James press release, "Teen Crisis in America: Rock Singer's New Book Offers Insight."

12. JustWorship.com Web site, http://www.justworship.com/ greekpraisewords.html.

13. Wikipedia Web site, http://en.wikipedia.org/wiki/Doxology.

14. Wright, N. T., *Simply Christian: Why Christianity Makes Sense* (New York: HarperOne, 2006).

15. James Strong, *A Concise Dictionary of the Words in the Hebrew Bible* (Nashville, TN: Abingdon Press, 1975), 102.

16. Rebecca St. James, Matt Bronleewe © 2005 Up in the Mix Music/Rambuka Music (BMI), admin by EMI CMG Publishing/ Songs of Windswept (BMI).

17. Rehoboth Farm Web site, http://rehobothfarm.blogspot .com/2007/11/art-as-reflection-of-mans-heart.html.

18. Rebecca St. James, Rob Hawkins © 2005 Up in the Mix Music/ Rambuka Music (BMI)/Meadowgreen Music Company (ASCAP), admin by EMI CMG Publishing.

19. Shane Claiborne, *The Irresistible Revolution: Living as an Ordinary Radical* (Grand Rapids: Zondervan, 2006).

About the Authors

Australian-born Rebecca St. James is both a Grammy Award winner and multiple Dove Award recipient, with international success that has driven her record sales into the millions. In January 2008, she was named "Favorite Female Artist" in Contemporary Christian Music by readers of *CCM Magazine* for the seventh consecutive year. Rebecca also won "Best Female Artist of 2007" from one of Christian music's highest traffic music sites—Christianitytoday.com—her fifth consecutive year to be given this honor. She has received RIAA certified gold album awards for two of her best-selling album projects: *God*, which was certified gold in 2005; and her Grammy Award–winning album *Pray*, which was certified in 2006.

Her signature blend of modern pop/rock sensibilities and lyrics of unwavering devotion have blazed the way to seventeen Top 10 singles—nine of which reached the #1 spot on the charts. *CRW Magazine* named Rebecca to the list of the "50 Most Influential People in Contemporary Music," and Crosswalk.com has recognized her as one of the "Top 50 Evangelical Leaders under Age 40." Her interests in acting have found her involved in several film productions and voicing the character of Hope the Angel in the VeggieTales best-selling DVD production *The Easter Carol*. Known for her passionate involvement in youth-related ministries, Rebecca is also an in-demand speaker and best-selling author. You can read more about Rebecca on her official Web site: www.rsjames.com; or on her MySpace page: www.myspace.com/rebeccastjames.

This is the fourth book Dale Reeves has written with Rebecca St. James. A former youth pastor, Dale traveled as a journalist with the contemporary Christian band Audio Adrenaline. Dale and his wife live in Mason, Ohio, scrapbook together, and have two college-age daughters.

If you liked *Pure*,
you'll love

Sister Freaks

Bestselling author and award-winning singer Rebecca St. James brings together a group of inspirational true stories about young women who gave their all for Jesus. Around the world, every day, these women are boldly putting themselves forth as believers—regardless of the cost. Sometimes they suffer for it, but they never waver in their belief that God has called them to serve Him.

Sister Freaks profiles both contemporary women and historical figures—from Joan of Arc to a Midwest high school student to an Olympic athlete. Their stories are sometimes extreme but always inspiring. Divided into thirteen weeks, the book features five profiles for each week, thought-provoking questions, and space for journaling.

Rebecca St. James has inspired thousands with her music. Now she empowers them with these very real, godly role models in whose footsteps they can follow.

Available now wherever books are sold.